Locomotive
Weathering Projects

Tim Shackleton

Ian Allan
PUBLISHING

First published 2015

ISBN 978 0 7110 3813 4

Published by Ian Allan Publishing Ltd, Addlestone, Surrey, KT15 2SF.

Printed in Great Britain

Visit the Ian Allan Publishing website at www.ianallanpublishing.com

Title page: Railway modelling is about doing the essentials well. If your track looks good and the stock is believable, then everything starts to fall into place. Weathering has a part to play, but so too do reliable operation, convincing scenics and imaginative presentation. The outward appearance of your models and the way they are finished is just one element among many, but it is usually the first anyone sees of a layout, whatever the scale.

CONTENTS

Acknowledgements

Books and magazines are not created in isolation – the author is usually at the mercy of a loosely-knit team of friends, advisors, fellow modellers, hangers-on and people he happens to know, all of whom will have their say at some stage. Among those who've directly or indirectly had a hand in the present production are Bob Barlow, Mick Bonwick, David Brandreth, Alex Duckworth, Chris Gibbon, John Gowers, Nick Grant, Brian Hanson, Bob Hetherington, Pete Hill, Tim Horn, Chris Langdon, Alex Medwell and Lisa Munro of The Airbrush Company, Martin Ray, Mick Simpson, Tony Sissons, John Sutton, Tim Watson, James Wells, Alan Whitehouse and Mike Wild. I thank them all for their friendship and for not always saying what I might have liked them to say.

Introduction

Right: How attitudes have changed – I weathered this Hornby 'Q1' as a demonstration piece at Pendon Museum, an institution once seen as the bastion of hair-shirted rivet-counting. The exceptional quality of today's RTR models renders them not just acceptable to finescale modellers, but as the preferred route of many. At the same time high-quality weathering – once seen as a black art – is increasingly finding a place in the mainstream.

Weathering has become an integral part of railway modelling in a way that scarcely seemed possible 20 years ago. In magazines, at exhibitions and in people's homes it's become rare to see layouts that show no evidence of any attempt to create a realistic, lived-in finish. A wide range of over-the-counter weathering products is now on the market, you can find a vast and ever-growing library of reference material in print and online, and just about the only thing you can't buy is the ability to look at the physical condition of a real-life locomotive and translate what you see into miniature form. Even that's not strictly true – you can take courses on the subject at places such as Missenden Abbey and Pendon Museum, where they have proved very popular. I know this because I teach them.

Weathering doesn't stand still. As one of the least fashionable people I know, I'm not keen on innovation for its own sake, but I do find myself looking back over the considerable body of material I've generated on the subject even in the last five or six years – in books, magazines and DVD programmes – and realise that my approach is constantly evolving. I might read something that sets me thinking, or some new products come my way, or I may just fancy trying something different. If nothing else, this catholic approach helps to demonstrate that there is no one sure-fire way to weather model locomotives that trumps all others. In fact there are many, some of which I've tried and some of which I've yet to hear about.

Left: As with so many aspects of modelling, Pendon led the way when it came to the naturalistic presentation of models. Now 50 years old, the Dartmoor scene – viewed here from the operator's position – has lost none of its capacity to inspire. Everything in view has been sympathetically weathered and even the gently fading colours somehow seem appropriate.

Right: Muted, naturalistic colours on Coldfair Green, the P4 layout of the Scalefour Society's Norfolk and Suffolk Area Group. The BTH Bo-Bo harmonises beautifully with its surroundings – no one element stands out even though the layout is the work of several hands. Everything has been thought through consistently from a visual perspective.

This present book gathers together a number of recent projects in the now-familiar step-by-step form, which I think is the best way of demonstrating the subject to learners. Most feature ready-to-run models, not just because this is what most people will be working with but because I am starting to run out of hand-built locomotives to use as weathering projects. Weathering a locomotive is a few hours' work, a weekend at most. A build is weeks or even months of intensive modelling time, and the higher up the evolutionary ladder you go, the longer it takes. I wonder if this is why those who build specimen models of locomotives for their own sake, and who don't have layouts to run them on, often prefer to finish them in immaculate museum-piece condition. Maybe they feel that presenting showcase models in an authentic external state – which may not mean dirty, far from it – may be a step too far, just as it is for the RTR collectors who never take their models out of their boxes.

So what are our priorities? What do people need to know about weathering? Most of the questions I'm asked relate to choice of equipment, to the materials I use and the way I use them. We'll deal with them next – and consider them as an integral part of each project. But dig a little deeper, and I often sense a touch of anxiety lurking there – the fear of things going wrong, of making disastrous mistakes, of good models ruined. So people become hesitant, handling an airbrush as if it were a 10-foot cobra. It's easy for me to say don't worry, just relax and enjoy yourself – but that's what you have to learn to do. If it's any comfort for first-timers, of whom I've taught a great many, I've never seen anyone go horrifically awry in the initial stages. I've seen early efforts from learners that weren't particularly good, but that's how it usually is in any creative endeavour – unless you happen to be naturally gifted, you just have to plug away at it, learning from your mistakes and looking at your work with a critical eye. The vast majority of first-timers, I find, are usually more than encouraged by their first attempts and improvement quickly follows.

Left: Modelling, to me, is all about creating atmosphere and the feeling that – if only for a moment – we could be looking at the real thing. A DMU for Ipswich departs from Coldfair Green in a scene that perfectly captures the Suffolk landscape where I live. The weathering of the Cravens unit – and of the trackwork and structures for that matter – is part of a much broader, integrated canvas.

Above: Why weather your models? Ixion's 7mm scale Kerr Stuart railmotor is extremely attractive, but in its pre-coloured plastic it looks more than a little toy-like. Even the preserved example in Australia isn't quite so unblemished and out-of-the-box.

Above: The locomotive section and carriage underframe have been scruffed up, the roof has been soot-blackened and the matchboarded sides painted in 'varnished wood' shades. It's all routine stuff but what a difference it makes to the believability of the model.

Right: I rarely finish kit-built or RTR-converted locos in ex-works condition, especially if they're going to be heavily weathered. I've done a lot of very obvious surgery on this Bachmann 'V2' body, which has been fitted with a Branchlines chassis and the tender from a 'J39'. It looks a mess – but it will all be covered by weathering.

Below: Even though the weathering is only 75% complete, the scars of the 'V2' are well hidden and the lined-green locomotive is perfectly matched with the black tender. I simply don't see the point of repainting the latter, still less lining it out. Weathering can't turn a poor model into a masterpiece but it can hide many sins.

Left: I saw a great many 'Jinties' in BR days, but none that looked like this. I am very cautious about using preserved locomotives as any kind of example or inspiration, but appreciate the needs of modellers who never saw the steam era. Personally I find it difficult to model anything that I haven't experienced for myself.

Right: From a weathering point of view I don't find much to excite me in the well-polished locomotives working on preserved railways, but just occasionally, when standards slide a little, they enable me to connect with my recollections of the real thing. The smokebox of this much-travelled 'N7' 0-6-2T is an object lesson in shades of brown, grey and black.

Below: I connect a lot more readily with the current railway scene, which I've always followed. Although the motive power and a lot of the infrastructure have changed, much still remains and provides an endless source of fascination – as well as essential information on weathering. On 24 February 2014 Freightliner's No 66606 takes an Eastleigh-Bescot engineer's train through King's Sutton.

Above: Not everything on the railway weathers in the same way or even at the same rate, and contrast is an all-important tool for the modeller. Used sparingly, it can yield telling effects. Having unloaded at Drax power station, freshly repainted GBRf ex-'Euroshed' No 66751 works empty hoppers through Colton Junction on its way back to Tyne Coal Terminal on 9 July 2014.

Below: Even black and white photographs can yield a lot of information. Waiting to go off shed at Nine Elms one afternoon in April 1963, 'S15' 4-6-0 No 30509 looks full of animation. Although its paintwork is flat and grubby, the oily wheels and motionwork convey a sense of animation just as much as the drifting steam.

Left: Across town at Stratford on the same day, this forlorn line of stored 'Baby Deltics' looks inert and lifeless. Everything is dead matt and devoid of any hint of the shininess – oil patches, leaks, rub marks around the doors – that betokens a working unit. Unfortunately many model locomotives – steam as well as diesel – exhibit a similar all-over flat finish, which leaves them devoid of life.

Above: This is the kind of image that always inspires me – 'Q1' No 33019 at Guildford in low winter light in the early 1960s. It appears to be coaled with briquettes, but notice also the dribbles, leaks and patching. The 2-HAL in the background is another study in colour and texture.

Right: Dauntless *at Euston c1962. Note the tidal wave of brake block dust along the tender flanks – this is probably what the factory-applied weathering on RTR models is trying to simulate. Although in reasonable external condition, the 'Jubilee' merges effortlessly into its grubby surroundings.*

Above: BR hadn't a clue about keeping its early diesel and electric locomotives clean, and often seemed not to bother. Entering Liverpool Lime Street with a Plymouth-Liverpool train, the bright blue livery of Class AL1 Bo-Bo No E3017 makes it look pretty shabby. Today's private operators are far more aware of the marketing value of clean, reliable trains.

Equipment

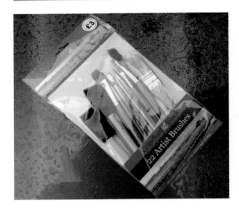

There are many ways of giving models a weathered finish. The simplest and cheapest would probably be to use a paintbrush and some kitchen roll – this is how I first weathered my Hornby-Dublo models more than 50 years ago. Or you could spend many hundreds of pounds on a quality airbrush, compressor and other spraying equipment – the choice is entirely yours.

Not all methods deliver the same results, however, and there is no right or wrong way to weather a model. Rather, it's a matter of combining different methods in a way that works for you. There are things you can do with an airbrush that cannot be achieved by any other means, while a simple stroke of a paintbrush – or not even that – may sometimes be the only way of gaining a particular effect.

The truth is that there's no one method of weathering, no one item of equipment, than can do everything or is intrinsically better than anything else. Instead, it's about using a combination of techniques – and an equivalent variety of equipment – to gain the results you want. The projects in this book will give you a good idea of the broad range of options that are possible.

An airbrush is often cited as the main piece of kit you need. I've used airbrushes for many years, and it's rare for me not to use one at some stage of a weathering project. On the other hand I know some very fine modellers who don't use airbrushes at all and rely entirely on simple paintbrushes and other means of putting paint and powders on their models. What they bring to the party, though, is a rare delicacy of touch and an instinctive eye for colour. Not

Right: With its 0.35mm nozzle, the gravity-feed Iwata TRN-2 can deliver fine mists and wafts of paint and is ideal for weathering provided you get the paint mix right. Although it's not expensive, it's a subtle airbrush and one that I use interchangeably with more upmarket designs. The double-action trigger is very easy to use. Pulling the trigger back releases first air, then paint in one smooth movement.

Left: The compact Iwata Revolution M1 is a single-action airbrush – you control the volume of paint delivery by adjusting the knurled nut at the rear of the barrel. Pressing the trigger on top of the airbrush releases air. Some people find single-action airbrushes easier to handle than the double-action type.

everyone has these skills, unfortunately, and people are often clumsy with a paintbrush in their hand. Using an airbrush rather than a paintbrush – though it still requires skill and practice – can help make up for a lack of artistic ability.

There are many different makes and types of airbrush, and a question I'm often asked is 'What should I buy?'. The simple answer is to buy the best you can possibly afford. Don't be tempted by online offers at too-good-to-be-true prices. You will not find a good airbrush for less than £50 (at 2015 values), and I'd be inclined to suggest £100 as the minimum spend – and that's for the airbrush alone, not for a package deal that also includes compressor, air line and other accessories. Budget-priced airbrushes – I have some of the more popular models in my Black Museum, which I use to frighten students – tend to be badly made, unreliable, perform indifferently and cause endless problems. If you can't afford the price of, say, an Iwata Neo – the best affordable airbrush ever made, bar none – then I'd suggest you explore other methods of painting your models, because they will invariably yield a better result and be far less frustrating.

I own and use a variety of designs from Iwata, Paasche and Badger – each make has its own characteristics. Choosing a good airbrush from a reliable brand opens the door to all kinds of weathering opportunities. This is purely and simply because they give you infinitely more control of paint and air delivery than a more basic design where you point and hope. A double-action airbrush, where the air and paint supplies are controlled simultaneously with the one trigger, is probably preferable, but when I'm simply putting a layer of paint on a model I often use a single-action design – it is, however, a very good one and one that I can adjust as precisely as any double-action airbrush.

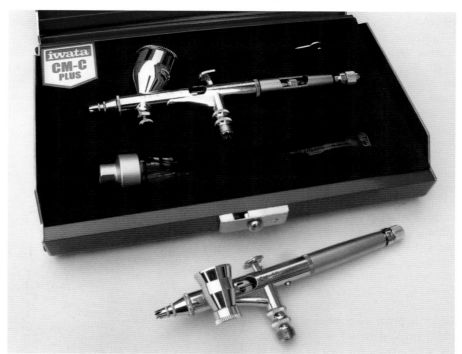

Left: Capable of the ultimate in finesse, the top-of-the-range Iwata Custom Micron is an airbrush for the experienced painter. I have two of them – the gravity-feed CM-C Plus with its 0.23mm nozzle and the side-cup CM-SB with an ultra-fine 0.18mm-diameter tip. Paint preparation is everything with these airbrushes, which can easily become choked by stray atoms of badly mixed pigment. One to gravitate towards, I feel...

Right: *High-end compressors such as my Iwata Smart Jet Pro are quiet, dependable and capable of delivering everything we could ask of them. The compressor automatically turns on when I press the airbrush trigger, providing instant air at the precise pressure I've set, and turns itself off again when the airbrush is not in use. Such sophistication, however, inevitably comes at a price.*

Left: *If you're on a budget you can't really go wrong with the reliable Aireco AS18-2, a great basic compressor for the hobbyist. Air supply is consistent and reliable, the pressure gauge actually works (unlike those on many economy compressors) and it doesn't run hot. Build quality is OK too, although it's not engineered for heavy, intensive use on a daily basis.*

You're on safer ground when it comes to air supply. Propellant cans are a fantastically expensive way to power your airbrush, and I haven't used them in years. A compressor is infinitely more economical and delivers a constantly available supply, but, here again, you get what you pay for. Once again, I'd set the bar at a figure of around £100, although there are some economically priced designs that are fine for the weekend sprayer. Above this amount you are far more likely get something well made, reliable, quiet and capable of adjustment in positive steps through a wide range of air pressures. Budget compressors tend in my experience to be noisy and a bit erratic in operation. The pressure valve, if fitted, is little more than a glorified on-off switch and offers little or no significant adjustment of air delivery; water traps are often equally ineffective, which is ironic given that cheap compressors – especially the old-fashioned diaphragm type – often run hot, leading to condensation in the air tube. An air tank will help even out the uneven, pulsing delivery endemic to diaphragm compressors, but with modern oil-less piston designs tanks are not really necessary.

Paints and powders

As my repertoire of techniques has expanded, I've increasingly gone over to using off-the-shelf, pre-mixed weathering products rather than preparing my own. I have no idea why this should be other than the fact that I have them to hand, so I feel I might as well use them. Paradoxically I still rely on the same three or four enamel colours I've always used, blending them into every weathering shade under the sun, but everything else is used pretty well as it comes. Well, sometimes…

So what do I use? I've never heard anyone – least of all myself – be critical of Humbrol and Revell enamel paints, LifeColor and Tamiya acrylics, or weathering products from makers such as MIG, Vallejo, AK-Interactive, Citadel and Wilder. If you see that as my endorsement of these brands at the expense of others that aren't named in this book, you may be right.

Enamels or acrylics? Both types of paint have good coverage, both are equally easy to apply by brush or airbrush, both are pretty durable when firmly set. Enamels dry more slowly, which is good if we want to work the still-wet paint to achieve particular post-application effects. You can do things with enamel paint for up to 24 hours afterwards. Acrylics are much faster-drying, which is great if we want to get the paint on and move quickly on to the next stage, but not so good if

Above: *I've been using Humbrol – and latterly Revell – enamels throughout my modelling lifetime and they are very much my preferred brands. They last almost indefinitely – this is probably the oldest one I have, a can of 'LNER Garter Blue' dating back to the early 1970s.*

Below: *I've always mixed my own colours with enamels but – for some inexplicable reason (laziness?) – I generally use pre-mixed acrylic colours, particularly these boxed sets from LifeColor, which contain virtually all the weathering shades we need.*

we want to play around with it. Therefore I use both, depending on circumstances. You cannot physically mix oil-based and water-based paints, but there is no problem about layering one on top of the other.

The subtlest effects of all, however, come not from a £350 airbrush but from weathering powders. Using tiny amounts in very controlled applications, it's possible to create all manner of nuances and shadings that would be impossible by any other means. I use powders in conjunction with other media, primarily paint, and rarely if ever employ weathering powders alone – which is not to say it can't be done. My

kind of finishing is all about building up layers – paint on top of powder on top of paint washes on top of more paint – because this is exactly how it works on the real thing. Surfaces rust, coats of paint fade, dirt builds up on top of it, water runs down and washes some of the grime away and so on and so on. It's a complicated, multi-faceted process that is far more involving (and satisfying to create) than simply applying a single airbrushed coat of weathering.

Working conditions

Making and painting models is a classic kitchen-table hobby. You don't need a workshop or studio, just a bit of common sense. Paint fumes can be damaging to health, especially when sprayed, so I like to work outdoors if I can, and indoors with a spray booth or extractor if I can't. If I'm just putting on a quick coat of paint, a respirator mask does the trick.

Thus protected, I have no problems with any of the solvent thinners I use – white spirit for enamels, isopropyl alcohol for acrylics. The additives in some of the proprietary thinners sold in model shops for use with enamel paints – as often as not in tins – tend to be very pungent and give me a headache. I never use cellulose-based paints these days.

You need to work in good light, and with plenty of clear space around you. An area about the size of a mouse mat isn't sufficient. Make sure all the tops are

Above: Box of tricks: these are some of the more specialised products I use, from makers such as Adam Wilder, AK-Interactive and MIG. As well as assorted washes, weathering powders and filters, there are also tubes of artists' gouache and oil colour.

Right: Domestic arrangements. From left to right: daylight lamp; spray booth with shelf; 12-inch painting turntable; airbrushes (with quick-release valves on air lines) on adjustable stand; cleaning station; twin compressor (Iwata Power Jet Pro). Everything is within easy reach and – equally importantly – all the tops are on the bottles.

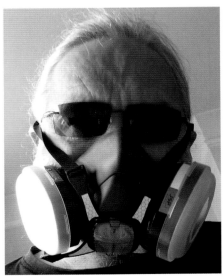

on your paints and powders, and be especially vigilant when you swing your painting turntable round.

I use vibration-free piston compressors so I can have my air supply standing on the work surface next to me, which makes it easy to adjust the pressure. Note than when I suggest a typical figure of 25-28psi for spraying enamels, and 18-20psi for acrylics, we are talking about the pressure reading on the dial when the airbrush is actually in use. When you aren't spraying, the standing pressure will be significantly higher – in other words, to obtain a working pressure of 20psi you need to set the pressure regulator to around 30psi or more. It's simple enough, but it's amazing how many people set their compressors to the lower figure and wonder why the paint isn't fully atomised.

Weathering is or can be messy, so you need kitchen roll or towels to hand to wipe up the inevitable spills. Once you've tipped the contents of the colour cup all over your work surface you will buy a proper stand for your airbrush. A cleaning station is a wise investment, enabling you to get rid of surplus paint or thinners without risk of spills or unpleasant fumes. Neither of these accessories is expensive and, as modellers seem to like buying things, they will prove a wise and very useful investment over time.

Above: A good respirator mask is important if you intend to spray for more than a couple of minutes and don't have access to an extractor. Disposable dust masks are worse than useless in this context – they lull you into a false sense of security.

FAQs

Will weathering my models gum up the works and obscure the detail?
Of course it won't, at least with the minimal quantities of paint that are necessary to create convincing weathering effects. Restraint and delicacy of touch are the key to success in this area, so the amount of paint we put on is tiny. But if you're ridiculously heavy-handed, and set out with the deliberate intention of putting on absurdly thick layers of paint, then there's always a faint risk.

What if it all goes pear-shaped and my models are ruined?
I have never known this happen, even with outright beginners. In the worst-case scenario you can dunk the model in a bath of thinners and scrub it clean – but this has never been necessary in my experience. True, your first attempts may not be very good, but that's all part of the learning curve. To be on the safe side, practice first on cast-offs and other models that don't matter.

I feel anxious about making a start on weathering – so I keep putting it off.
It's only natural that you should feel edgy, but there really is nothing to worry about. The worst that can happen is that the results aren't as good as you might have hoped – but you can always try a bit harder next time. Pretty well all my

Right: A film of paint a few atoms thick is not going to provide much of an obstacle to a locomotive mechanism capable of hauling a 50-wagon freight.

students are a little nervous at first, but once you get into the swing of things all that vanishes and you start to enjoy yourself.

Should I buy a cheap airbrush first, before committing myself? Is that a good way to learn?
I wouldn't bother. The only thing you will learn with a cheap airbrush is how to appreciate a good one when you finally get your hands on one, as you inevitably will. Budget airbrushes are incredibly limiting, unreliable and perform poorly. The absolute minimum spend on an airbrush should be £50, and I would think seriously about doubling this.

Do I need an airbrush at all?
If you already have a lot of artistic ability, and know how to apply paint sensitively, creatively and with a fair measure of control, then you may not necessarily need one. If like most people you have only limited skill with a paintbrush, a good airbrush will make life a lot simpler for you – certainly in terms of creating the subtle effects necessary in weathering.

Should I start off just using weathering powders? I can wash them off and start again if necessary.
Weathering powders have a greasy texture that makes them extremely difficult to remove. They have great value and can – with practice – produce incredibly subtle effects, but whether you can successfully weather an entire model with them is debatable. Normally I use them in conjunction with paint and other media.

How do you seal your weathering?
I don't. It isn't necessary – acrylic and enamel paints are hard-wearing enough as they are. Putting a sealing coat over weathering powders always affects their colour, destroying the effects you've been carefully building up. Besides, most of the weathering on a model locomotive is on areas we

Below: Don't be tempted by budget airbrushes like these. Carrying no discernible brand name, manufacturing quality is cheap and nasty, reliability questionable. You won't get convincing results with them, so why bother?

Right: I use
weathering powders
much as I use spices
in Indian cooking –
as a way of adding
flavour and a bit
of colour. On most
of my weathering
projects, however,
the basic groundwork
is always done in
paint.

don't handle, so what are we protecting it from? If the finish starts to wear, add a light coat of weathering over the top. LifeColor 'Burned Black' (UA 736) is a great colour for touching-in minor scuffs and abrasions – its neutral shade seems to become invisible.

What's the big secret?

There are several. Always look hard at the prototype and copy what you see – never make up weathering effects, or copy other people's models (except mine!). If using an airbrush, keep it scrupulously clean at all times. Beware of fumes and airborne paint particles, and take reasonable precautions. Always allow adequate drying times before handling your models, or adding further effects. Learn when to stop. Remember to clean the wheels afterwards!

Left: It's important to keep your airbrush meticulously clean at all times. These products are specifically formulated for airbrush maintenance. The soft foam mat is invaluable when dismantling your airbrush – it stops the parts rolling away!

Portfolio

Above: There's more than a hint of clean dirt around Bob Hetherington's demure Stockton & Darlington 2-4-0 Woodlands – sufficient to suggest that it's a working locomotive rather than a museum piece. Effective weathering of pre-Grouping models seems to be a rarity, especially in the larger scales.

Above: Grubbier still, Bob's scratchbuilt model of a Stockton & Darlington Railway banking engine gives, I feel, an accurate picture of the working railway in the Victorian era – and for many years after. Remember that pre-Grouping railways operated in a far dirtier environment than the one we've known in the last 40-50 years. There was no Clean Air Act, coal was the primary fuel, industry produced incredible levels of pollution, and we had none of today's sophisticated 'dirt-buster' cleaning agents.

Right: I wanted to finish my model of Huddersfield shed's ex-LYR 2-4-2T No 50725 as she looked immediately before withdrawal in 1958 – clean and presentable, but showing the evidence of a 62-year working life. Care and attention to detail are what counts with this kind of weathering – the methods and materials are almost incidental. Touches such as the polished spectacles, the red buffer-beam and the evidence of cleaning on the tank and bunker sides suggest this engine was well looked after. Sheds often singled out individual locomotives for particular attention, while others were left to fend for themselves. As a case in point, the local 'Austerities', Fowler 2-6-4Ts and Standard Class 5s were invariably filthy.

Above: This powerful-looking '72xx' 2-8-2T is very much in 'end-of-steam' condition, with corrosion evident on the bunker and smokebox and caked-on oil on the wheel centres. The motionwork, however, glistens with fresh oil, which helps to suggest that this Valleys workhorse has a few more miles to run yet before withdrawal.

Above: Even to someone accustomed to high-end models of American-outline articulated power, the Heljan Garratt is a staggering achievement. Sympathetic weathering helps bring out its strengths – out of the box, it's uncomfortably toy-like.

Above & Left: The bodywork of early diesels was absolutely swimming in oil, which attracted dirt and gradually created a thick and impenetrable layer of brownish filth. This Dapol model of No 10001 shows the effect, with oil leaking out of the engine-room doors and louvres and dribbling on to the bogies. On the real thing, holes had to be drilled at floor level to get rid of the excess lubricant thrown out by the prime mover.

Right: Diesel shunters tended to be more neglected than most. I built this P4 model of an Andrew Barclay 0-6-0DM from one of Mike Edge's kits. An all-pervasive oiliness is again a key feature, together with the steady build-up of dirt thrown up from the track and the locomotive's working environment.

Right: After a shopping, even 08s often looked clean, and this was my brief with this Hornby model. Dirt build-up is highly selective, concentrating on the oil filters, coupling rods and fuel tanks.

Below: In 7mm scale there is scope – and indeed a necessity – for highly detailed weathering. The bodywork of Western Ranger *is presentably clean but the running gear and side skirts are predictably smothered in an accumulation of road dirt, oil and spilled fuel, all carefully differentiated. The roof is slightly faded, and the panel lines picked out with colour washes.*

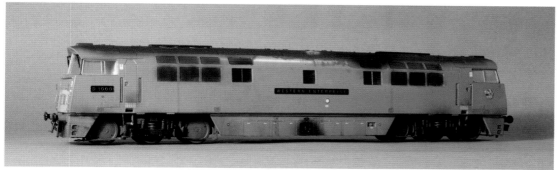

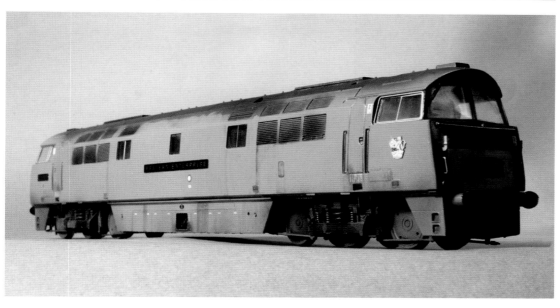

Left & Below left: Where it's appropriate I like to see a gloss finish on a locomotive. I think it's far better suited to an engine in this kind of halfway reasonable condition than the curiously dead semi-matt finish that many RTR manufacturers use as standard. Selective weathering of the critical areas – roof, bogies and engine-room grilles – has, together with an astute streak or two in the right place, produced a portrait of a unique locomotive. 'Westerns' could and did become extremely shabby – certainly in the Corporate Blue era – but in their heyday a lot of care was devoted to their appearance.

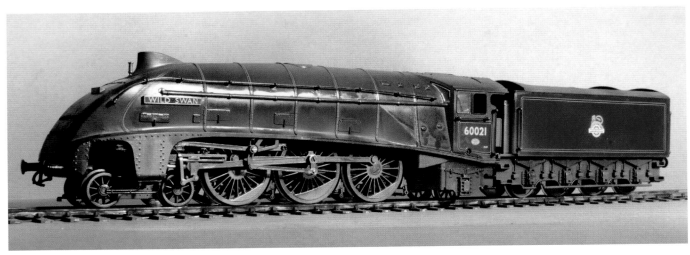

Above: An 'A4' 'Pacific' in classic East Coast condition for the 1950s – immaculate, but still looking every inch the working locomotive. It is quite a challenge to combine dirt build-up around the wheels and motion and the sooting along the top of the boiler with the oily-rag finish evident on the streamlined casing, cab and tender. Gleaming, but showing obvious signs of use, a top-link locomotive like Wild Swan looks nothing like an out-of-the-box model!

Above & Left: These two 'L1s' are as different as I could possibly make them. Work-weary RSH-built No 67777 is a Darlington-allocated engine that spent its whole life in the area. It has the large 10-inch numbers seen on many engines overhauled at North Road shops, and it also has the low (and very draughty) cab doors that were often the subject of complaints.

Fresh from overhaul at Darlington Works, No 67722 is a Westinghouse-braked example that will shortly be returning to its home shed, Bishop's Stortford, complete with a fresh coat of paint, the new post-1956 emblem and replacement full-height 'limousine' cab doors. The brightwork has been polished and the engine gleams like a new toy. For every loco in this kind of condition, you saw hundreds that looked like No 67777.

Left: Three Hornby 'Black Fives', all different in terms of detail, each weathered in a highly individual way. The variations are not enormous but to the discerning eye they represent an intriguing diversity.

Right: This close-up of a very natural-looking 'Black Five' is typical of these splendid go-anywhere, do-anything locomotives. If you were going round a depot in the late 1950s/early 1960s – and at Kingmoor or Crewe South, on a weekend, you could easily see 30 or 40 'Black Fives' among the 100-plus locos on shed – you wouldn't look twice at No 44668. This is a Hornby model that has been considerably upgraded with replacement components from Brassmasters and Alan Gibson.

Left and Below: Further variety on a pair of Hornby rebuilt 'Royal Scots'. *Royal Engineer* is in the kind of spruced-up condition often encountered in the 1950s, but *Cameronian* shows the neglect that was becoming increasingly common. Neither, however, is in any way an extreme example. Both were Holbeck engines at the time. *Royal Engineer* looks ready to head north over the Settle & Carlisle line with the 'Thames-Clyde Express' or the 'Waverley', but I've shown *Cameronian* in its final days as a freight loco and (famously) still with early-style BR symbol.

Above left & right: Similar but different (again): green-liveried D6 Whernside *is in the neglected, couldn't-care-less external condition that was typical of BR's expensive first-generation diesel traction. A change of livery to BR Corporate Blue hasn't done much for D186 either. Diesels could and sometimes did get a lot dirtier than this, but there comes a point in weathering a model when it just becomes overkill.*

Below & bottom: This is the deluxe version of the Hornby Duke of Gloucester *reworked to early 1960s condition with a BR1J tender and other modifications and detailing. I based the weathering on a couple of colour photographs of the engine, taken at Holyhead in 1962 – unusually, they showed both sides.*

Above & Top: I like commonplace and familiar locomotives, especially 'WD' 2-8-0s (and these days Class 66s). You have to know what something looks like before you can model it successfully. Although weathering techniques vary between the scales (in 2mm it is necessarily simplified and toned down), once you have a mental picture of what you want to achieve, transferring that vision into reality is largely a mechanical process.

Below: By the 1990s the paintwork of many first-generation diesels was getting pretty shabby and the tired Civil Engineer's 'Dutch' livery of No 37207 is no exception. I painted most of it by hand to get the right feel. The model is a much-altered Lima locomotive on a Dyna-Drive chassis.

Above: Portrait of an unwanted, uncared-for workhorse. The 650hp Paxman-engined Type 1s were very much a product of the steam era and they were treated no differently – just like many early BR diesels. I doubt if they were ever cleaned – why would they be? However, this was one of 48 members of the class that would find a new lease of life in industrial use.

Left: An out-of-the-box Bachmann Class 66 has been given a weathering treatment that exactly mirrors what I've seen on the prototype. The underframes of GBRf locos are as grubby as anyone else's but the bodysides seem to be washed down more frequently than other operators' locomotives, though there is usually a characteristic bow wave of weathering on the cabsides.

Left: This EWS '66' is quite a bit dirtier than GBRf's, as they usually are. The maroon livery shows up the dirt more than other operators' liveries. It's important to maintain continuity within your fleet because things like brake-block dust and oil stains never vary significantly in colour. I use all manner of different paints, powders, washes and filters, but they all come from a common palette.

Above & Right: I have been heavily into HO scale US model railroading for many years – specifically Class A western railroads of the 21st century. The challenge here is that locomotives weather very differently in California than they do in Britain – the colours are different, the weathering patterns are different, even the weathering products are formulated differently.

Above: *This is the largest locomotive I've ever weathered – an Aristocraft G scale (1:20) Alco A/B unit. It's far from being a true-scale model, but at 4 feet long it's pretty impressive. Even so, I reckon it took only two or three cupfuls of paint to achieve this effect.*

Below & Bottom: *Does Bachmann's Windhoff MPV classify as a locomotive or multiple unit? Either way, it makes for a fascinating model, especially when displaying the effects of chemical sprays along the prominent chassis side members. The modules and cabs, however, are still reasonably clean.*

CHAPTER

3

Projects

The essentials: a Stanier 2-6-4T

I basically start from scratch with every weathering project I undertake. Each is highly individual and in a sense unique – even when I'm weathering 30 or more of the same wagon, every one will have a distinctive identity all its own. No two models are ever quite alike.

At the same time there is a set of common or core elements, and what I'd like to do here with this Stanier 2-6-4T is to show the basics in action – a kind of default-setting weathering, if you like. I'll be employing tools and materials that I use all the time – in some of the later projects in this book, we'll be moving on to looking at more specialised products. I feel that getting a mastery of the basics is essential before you can make progress, and until you can use an airbrush and ordinary enamel (or acrylic) paints with the required degree of subtlety you are not going to scale the Olympic heights of weathering in a hurry. Here I'm using a very simple palette and equally basic techniques that essentially involve airbrushing on the paint, then taking much of it off again.

Despite being something of a demonstration piece, this is still a go-for-broke project as much as a gentle introduction to the art of weathering. There is no such thing as 'Weathering Lite' in my book. Putting paint on and then working it to create particular effects, adding layers of different colours, each barely distinguishable from the last, using powders and other media to complement paint, all the time looking closely at your subject – this is how weathering is done. Learn how to do the simple things properly, and afterwards all should be plain sailing.

Above: From a detail point of view the Hornby model is superb – one of the very best they have ever produced. The driving wheels are OK, but I changed the bogie and pony wheels to Alan Gibson examples, which give a much more finescale appearance. Etched screw couplings and a new identity are the only other alterations I made. To be sure of following the correct weathering patterns, however, I spent a lot of time studying colour photographs of these locomotives before I felt ready to make a start.

Right: All manner of special weathering preparations are available from the trade, some of which are very good and some of which, to be frank, are awful. You can do much of the work, however, with a handful of well-chosen enamel colours, and I think it's important that you master these before moving on.

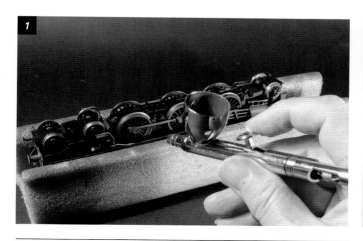

1: Since the locomotive will be weathered as a whole, there is no need to separate the chassis from the bodywork. In the initial stages, however, I prefer to begin the chassis weathering by inverting the loco in a foam cradle so I can spray from underneath. The airbrush is an Iwata Eclipse CS.

2: Don't forget to weather the underside of the buffers – it's surprising how often this is neglected. The paint mix I'm using is a familiar one of 60% 'Matt Black' (Revell 9), 25% 'Matt Leather' (Humbrol 62) and 15% 'Orange' (Revell 85), the latter to offset the greenish tinge that recent production runs of 'Matt Leather' have shown.

3: See how little paint is needed to create a weathered effect. It amounts to little more than a dusting over the Stanier's wheels. There is no danger of gumming up the valve gear with paint, although you will need to give the wheel treads a thorough cleaning after you've finished painting the locomotive.

4: With the loco the right way up, I can add more of the same colour to the bodysides as well as touching in any areas of the chassis that the airbrush has failed to penetrate. It's a good idea, at this stage, to add some more 'Matt Black' to the mix and go over selected areas such as the firebox and boiler to create subtly different colour tints.

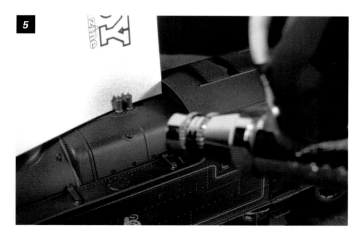

5: Brightwork is always annoying because it stands out like a sore thumb, and looks most unrealistic. You can hand-paint details such as the whistle and safety valves or you can stick with the airbrush, using a business card as a mask to stop overspray accumulating on the firebox. With a quality airbrush such as an Iwata you can come right in close to target particular areas.

6: To paint the smokebox I've made up a third, still darker version of the weathering mix to which I've added a touch of Humbrol Metal Cote 'Gunmetal' (27004). As the name suggests, this gives a convincing metallic sheen that replicates the finish often seen on real smokeboxes.

7: I've airbrushed some of the same mix on the wheel centres and motionwork, where it gives a good impression of oil build-up spilling out over the spokes through centrifugal force.

8: To create the effect of selective cleaning I've let the enamel paint dry for half an hour or so, and now I've started to take some of it off, using a flat half-inch brush lightly dampened with white spirit. There's plenty of grime still remaining, though, in areas that the cleaner's rag hasn't reached. This method gives you great control over the degree of cleanliness/dirtiness your loco exhibits.

9: You soon learn that the less paint you put on to begin with, the less there is to take off. A token effort was usually made to clean the buffer-beams, and this is great fun to reproduce in miniature. One reason I prefer enamels over acrylics in this kind of application is that the latter dry far too quickly. Unless you wash them off instantaneously, they are very difficult to remove and the resulting 'scrubbed' effect isn't what we want at all. You can use retarders to slow down drying time, but I usually find it's easier to use enamels in the first place.

10: I've put my airbrush down and now I'm going over to weathering powders to add the detail touches. These give incredibly subtle effects and form an essential component of my weathering repertoire. I've chosen colours that harmonise with the palette of enamel and acrylic paints that I use on most of my weathering projects. Quality ranges such as MIG, LifeColor and AK-Interactive are surprisingly consistent in coloration, other makes less so.

11: *I am very circumspect about using the more strident rust shades – to look plausible in 4mm scale I think they're best toned down with a darker colour. Here I'm adding a splash or two of 'Dark Mud' (P033) and 'Track Brown' (P414) to the brake gear – particles from iron brake blocks liberally coat parts of the underframe and start to rust.*

12: *I've put a much lighter colour – MIG 'Rubble Dust' (P234) – on to the front platform to represent ash residue from the smokebox char thrown out during servicing.*

13: *Now for some 'Black Smoke' (P023) on the sides of the smokebox to vary the tone. Weathering is rarely even, but the patchiness is subtle, and easily overdone.*

14: *The cab roof is similarly treated, with tints of 'Dark Mud' (P033) and 'Industrial City Dirt' (P039) here and there. I brush the powder downwards off the roof to mimic the effect of rainwater.*

15: *The insides of coal bunkers are always heavily rusted, on tank and tender locomotives alike. Here I am using a mixture of 'Dark Mud' and 'Track Brown' to create a subtle variety. Only tiny quantities of powder are needed – if you put too much on, you can try and neutralise it with black or, if that fails, airbrush it out.*

16: I have tried many methods of reproducing oily valve gear and I think AK-Interactive's 'Fuel Stains' (AK 025) is far and away the best. A thick, treacly enamel-based paint, it smells like household gloss and for best effect you should brush it on liberally. There is no risk of gumming up the works.

17: Even when the core of the work is done, detail weathering adds the final touches. Note the oil spills around the lubricator, grease spots on the buffers, patches of corrosion around the steam fittings and tank fillers – all done using the same materials as before.

18: The outcome: a convincing depiction of a working steam locomotive, not especially clean but not particularly dirty either.

19: Cleaners were always in short supply during the BR era and increasingly scant attention was paid to what was once seen as an essential task. Often locomotives would be only partially cleaned before going back into service. Anything that was hard to reach, such as the boiler or the bunker rear, would be conveniently forgotten.

Papyrus: a well-cleaned express locomotive in 2mm scale

Until a few years ago I'd never done any weathering in 2mm scale – or anything smaller than HO, come to that. These days, with the encouragement of friends in the 2mm world, I'm finding it an increasingly fascinating scale in which to work. Like a miniature portrait, success depends entirely on careful application and the determined omission of anything that's either non-essential or carries the risk of being overcooked.

The actual putting on of paint and powder isn't difficult – it's the delicacy of touch and the degree of self-control that constitutes the essential features of weathering in this scale. You need to be sparing with everything from your brushstrokes to your colour palette – three or four weathering shades will be more than adequate, otherwise it all starts to look a little forced. Technique is equally economical and I don't make a great deal of use of airbrushes in 2mm work – although I feel they're still the best way of doing the roofs of coaching stock and diesel or electric locomotives. Pretty well everything else can be done by hand. Good-quality paintbrushes, however, are important – at this scale a stray hair looks like a cable run.

This might be a good point to say something about scale colour. Colour scales in proportion to distance, which means that, from normal viewing angles, this particular model of *Papyrus* needs to be a lot less green than Dapol make it – in tone, I feel the shade as it stands would be better suited to a 7mm scale model. The colour intensity of ready-mixed paints, powders and other media, moreover, is generally balanced to meet the needs of armour and aviation modellers working in 1/48 scale or thereabouts. While you can get away with them in 4mm scale, if you're using ready-mixed paints in 2mm scale they will need significant re-evaluation and very probably reduction if they're to look plausible.

Above: Dapol's N gauge model of Papyrus *is an incredible production, with refinements and levels of detail hitherto associated only with high-end 4mm scale RTR models. With only a little attention from Tim Watson – and an extra touch or two of lining from Ian Rathbone – it's already good enough for the Model Railway Club's spectacular model of the approaches to King's Cross, 'Copenhagen Fields'.*

1: One of my main criticisms of N gauge manufacturers, however, is that the colours are far too bright and intense. This is certainly true of Papyrus, where the interpretation of Doncaster green would be better suited to a 7mm scale model. The first stage was, therefore, to tone it down. I used a fine mist of a ComArt filter called 'Light Dust', breathed on from close in with an Iwata HP-SB airbrush.

2: This before-and-after image shows how the bilious green of the loco body has been toned right back on the tender. The intensity of the colour is now far more plausible and in scale.

3: To discolour the paintwork and bring out the relief detail I used MIG's 'Dark Wash', brushed on by hand in small quantities. There are plenty of pictures showing Gresley 'Pacifics' in pre-war days looking none too clean – only a small proportion could be described as immaculate.

4: The result of that brushwork is some subtle staining, with dirt collecting in out-of-the-way places. This technique works well in all scales. Be careful, though, not to allow it to collect and dry behind the handrails, which really gives the game away. I've also put an initial wash of colour over the motionwork, as this is rarely clean, even on a highly polished locomotive.

5: Scaling down colour in 2mm means that things need to be a lot lighter than we perhaps imagine them to be. Pure black is or should be unknown, so I've brushed some pale-coloured MIG weathering powder on to areas that reflect the sky, such as the running plate and cab roof. I used 'Industrial City Dirt' (P039), which is a neutral beige-grey shade. I've brushed it on (and brushed it off again) in a slightly patchy manner that helps to break up the solid black of the plastic moulding.

6: To add more powder to the areas below the footplate, as well as the tender frames and rear well, I used 'Dark Mud' (P033) let down here and there with a hint of 'Black Smoke' (P023). To avoid swamping the model when using weathering powders, you always have to be niggardly with quantities, and this is especially true in 2mm scale.

7: *Everything has been brought down in tone to be in proportion with the green bodywork, which is the first thing that catches the eye. Now* Papyrus *looks a lot more plausible, yet it's taken very little work to achieve this effect. The combination of dark wash and weathering powders is perfect for 2mm modelling. I find an airbrush is very far from essential here, but if you're going to use one in this scale it has to be a good make. Budget airbrushes are too crude and the resulting scattergun effect looks dreadful.*

8: *The next stage is to add some sheen to the matt-finish bodywork, for which Johnson's Klear is the obvious choice. It is now sold as Pledge Multi-surface Wax which has a different smell and a slight colour tinge but, having used them side by side, I find there is no practical difference whatsoever between the old and new formulations. It is best brushed on with the biggest paintbrush you have, using vertical strokes. A slight patchiness works well on a weathered loco, whatever the scale – it seems to suggest a rippling in the metalwork, which is prototypical.*

9: *I've coaled up the tender using fine dust that I'd been using on 4mm scale MGR wagons, applied over a coat of gloss black paint and sealed with hairspray. There is always some overspill around the tank filler.*

10: Even in 2mm scale it's always a good plan to make a feature of the 'living' parts of a locomotive, such as the rubbing marks and abrasions where the crew climb in and out of the cab. There is caked-on oil – more 'Black Smoke' weathering powder – around the axleboxes, while the over-bright whistle and safety valves have been toned down.

11: The amount of work I've put in hasn't been vast, but it's all been very carefully considered. Everything is there for a reason and, while nothing has been left out, my focus has been on getting the essentials right. The key point about modelling in 2mm scale is that you put the detail where it can be seen, and I think that's true of weathering too.

12: Now that we have N gauge RTR of this kind of quality, I think it's important that we make the most of the way the models are finished so the overall standard can be pushed still further. I sent this image to an experienced modeller, telling him it was a 7mm loco. I'm pretty sure he believed me…

Weathering a 'Pacer'

My impression is that, over the last 20 years, passenger trains have become a lot cleaner than they were at the tail end of the British Rail era. Intensively used long-distance stock on the East and West Coast Main Lines may sometimes appear a little grubby – especially in winter – but secondary services are, for the most part, delivered by trains that are an awful lot smarter than they used to be.

The nadir for me was a 1993 journey in a Class 153 'Bubble Car' from Swansea through Llanelli and Carmarthen and out on to the Pembroke branch. It took ages and the unit was absolutely filthy, inside and out – even if you had a seat with a full set of cushions you could hardly see out of the windows. This, moreover, was midsummer.

Customer-facing business thinking has largely relegated that kind of experience to the dustbin of history. As a photographer, one of the benefits that privatisation has brought to me is the opportunity to see and capture a wide variety of clean, colourful units at work. Before this I hardly ever photographed them, but now they've brought a renewed focus of interest in the railway scene and an enhancement of my enjoyment of a few hours by the lineside. This new-found enthusiasm has also passed through into my modelling.

Left: *The Realtrack Models Class 144 is one of the best RTR products to be released in recent years, all the more so for being a first-time effort from a small two-man business. It has a mass of detailing – especially below floor level – that sympathetic light weathering will help to bring out.*

1: With the units upended in a foam cradle, I airbrushed a thin mist of LifeColor 'Frame Dirt' (UA 719) acrylic paint over the chassis, using an Iwata Eclipse CS. To stop overspray landing on the bodysides I used a length of thin card as a mask.

2: The next stage was to darken some areas of the underframe with hints of 'Burned Black' (UA 736). Once again a spray mask is advisable.

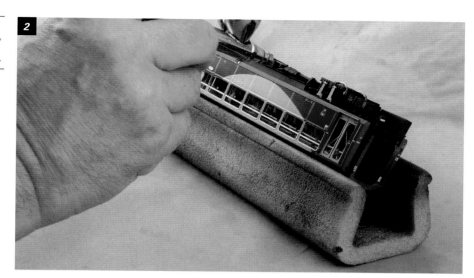

3: The third colour application is a 20:80 mix of 'Frame Dirt' and 'Brake Dust' (UA 724). The precise control of the Iwata airbrush enables me to target particular areas, building up subtly modulated underframe colours based on prototype observation.

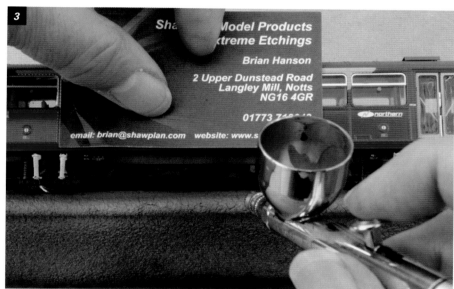

4: Using a colour wash allows you to vary the degree of weathering on the sides – from a light accumulation to a midwinter coat of filth. I began (lower vehicle) by adding a dark wash of grey-brown enamel to the lines of rivets, then immediately taking most of it off again, using a brush moistened with white spirit and working it along the body. This leaves a subtle pattern of 'ingrained dirt' in recessed areas, as in the upper vehicle. My wash was made up of 70% 'Matt Black' (Revell 8), 20% 'Matt Leather' (Humbrol 62) and 10% 'Orange' (Revell 85) let down with a lot of white spirit.

5: Having washed off most of the colour to leave subtle streaks, I've dabbed a touch of MIG 'Black Smoke' weathering powder into the door recesses and other areas where dirt would accumulate. These units are cleaned pretty regularly so dirt build-up is never very heavy in summer, but in winter the sides are liberally caked with a brownish filth that looks very much like factory-applied weathering. To replicate this, just use more wash and don't take so much of it off.

6: To gain inspiration for the roof weathering I went out and photographed real Class 144s from a road bridge over a deep cutting. Dirt build-up varies between units, but follows consistent patterns. The first step was to lightly airbrush 'Burned Black' around the eaves, leaving the peak of the roof untouched.

7: Having left the acrylic paint to harden overnight, I brushed some broad streaks of MIG 'Dark Wash' enamel across the roof, then took them off with white spirit, leaving a random pattern of lateral streaks to mimic rainwater. To be effective the result should be barely visible, but still noticeable.

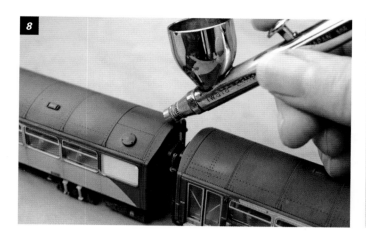

8: Finally I airbrushed some Revell 'Anthracite' (9) on the roof around the exhaust outlets, to represent the heavy sooting that always builds up here. Again, it's not all that different from the general roof discoloration, but it all adds to the subtlety of the overall effect.

9: The roof is no longer one solid colour, but a subtly varied range of shades – the original roof colour, the darker tone around the eaves, the exhaust sooting and the barely discernible streaks running down towards the rainstrips.

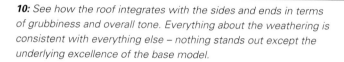

10: See how the roof integrates with the sides and ends in terms of grubbiness and overall tone. Everything about the weathering is consistent with everything else – nothing stands out except the underlying excellence of the base model.

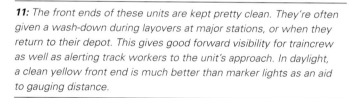

11: The front ends of these units are kept pretty clean. They're often given a wash-down during layovers at major stations, or when they return to their depot. This gives good forward visibility for traincrew as well as alerting track workers to the unit's approach. In daylight, a clean yellow front end is much better than marker lights as an aid to gauging distance.

Transition-era diesels

On the whole, the diesel and electric traction of the green-livery era (roughly 1957 to 1970) soon became as badly neglected as any steam locomotive, at least in terms of its outward appearance. At depot level, BR didn't really seem to know what to do with its new fleet. Mechanical cleaning plants were few and far between and while slab-sided designs such as the English Electric Type 4s should in theory have been easy to clean, in practice they were just as filthy as those locomotive classes whose bodysides were a mass of dirt-attracting louvres, grilles and panels. BR had trouble enough recruiting maintenance staff for the new generation of motive power, and engine cleaners were by then in painfully short supply – so on the whole they didn't bother. Most locomotives only got cleaned when they went for major overhaul.

The Brush Type 2s were typical of their era. They were attractive-looking engines and the livery elements were well chosen. As exclusively Eastern Region engines, a lot of them were allocated to depots with washing facilities such as Stratford, Finsbury Park and Tinsley, but their appearance could quickly become neglected. As with most first-generation diesels, there was usually quite a bit of shine about them, but a persistent problem – never really cured – was oil leakage from the engine room, which seeped out over the lower bodysides right where the broad cream band could emphasise it most. The front ends, on the whole, were kept clean because railwaymen were mindful of the safety aspects of the yellow warning panel, which enabled track workers to gauge the distance and speed of approaching trains far better than high-intensity headlights. This consideration still applies today, which is why it is rare to see a locomotive or unit with a grubby warning panel.

Above: For a design dating back almost 50 years, the styling of the Brush Type 2 continues to wear well. Straight out of the box, Heljan's 7mm scale model faithfully captures its essential qualities.

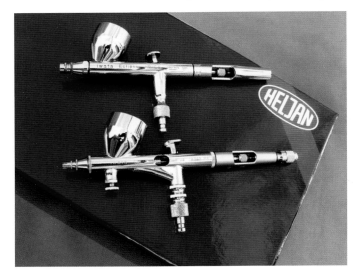

Left: These are the airbrushes I chose to use for this project – the Iwata Eclipse CS (above) and the Iwata CM-C Plus. The latter is, quite simply, the best airbrush I've ever used, being capable of incredible levels of delicacy.

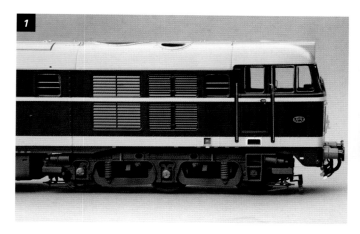

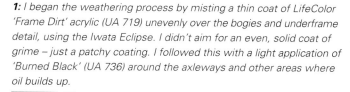

1: I began the weathering process by misting a thin coat of LifeColor 'Frame Dirt' acrylic (UA 719) unevenly over the bogies and underframe detail, using the Iwata Eclipse. I didn't aim for an even, solid coat of grime – just a patchy coating. I followed this with a light application of 'Burned Black' (UA 736) around the axleways and other areas where oil builds up.

2: Oil got everywhere on these early diesels and I intensified the effect using Tamiya 'Flat Black' (XF1), again applied with the Eclipse CS at a pressure of around 18psi. Before the paint dried – with acrylics, this doesn't take very long – I wiped the yellow axlebox covers clean using a brush dipped in isopropyl alcohol-based airbrush cleaner.

3: The roof was weathered with a combination of 'Burned Black' and 'Roof Dirt' (UA 722), with the former predominating. I used colour photographs of green-liveried Brush Type 2s as my guide, copying the specific areas where the exhaust sooting built up.

4: 'Flat Black' is used to emphasise the areas around the exhaust ports. This is one of the few occasions where I'll use a neat matt black on a model, rather than modulating it slightly with brown or grey. The Iwata CM-C Plus comes into its own in creating these subtle transitions, but the grab handles are best hand-painted with 'Burned Black', using a fine No 0 brush.

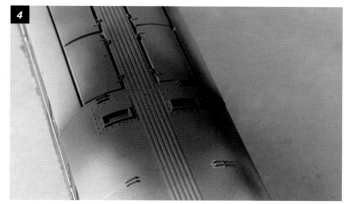

5: Once the acrylic paints on the roof were dry, I brush-painted a dark grey-brown enamel wash over the remaining areas that were still in their factory finish. I could have mixed my own, but here I used Adam Wilder's 'Grey Shadow Wash' (NL 04). Working it into barely discernible vertical streaks created a subtle texture that mimics rain marks.

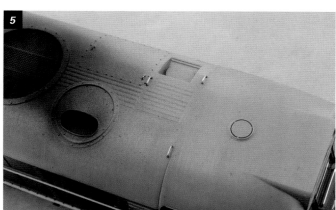

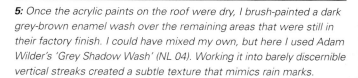

6: *Roof detail is important, and should be emphasised – we mostly see our models from above. I've run a thin pin wash of Wilder 'Black Smoke Wash' (NL 01) along all the panel lines, then added further airbrushed streaks of 'Burned Black' acrylic sprayed though a slit cut in a business card held close to the roof.*

7: *The oil accumulating on the bodyside ventilation grilles attracts dirt, but the livery colour will still show through. I painted these areas with Wilder 'Dark Rainmark Wash' (NL 32), allowing it to settle in the louvres before overspraying with a very light coat of 'Burned Black'. Again, the precise targeting and level of control possible with a sophisticated airbrush like the Iwata CM-C makes this easy to achieve.*

8: *Throughout their lives the Brush Type 2s suffered from oil accumulating on the engine room floor and seeping out through the bodysides – the cream band could hardly have been worse positioned in that respect, since it emphasised the leaks. The oil spills are individually hand-painted using a No 0 brush and a combination of Humbrol 'Satin Black' enamel (No 85) and AK-Interactive's 'Fuel Stains' (AK 025).*

9: Using a fine-pointed brush I've picked out all the seam lines and panelling with MIG 'Dark Wash' (P220) to emphasise the relief detail and create false shadows. This kind of treatment is virtually mandatory for 7mm models, and even in the smaller scales has a noticeable effect – it seems to tighten up all the detail.

10: Study the variety of weathering effects that I've built up on the roof, and how they complement the bodysides. There are various kinds and colours of streaks, some heavy sooting around the exhaust outlets, a general discoloration around the fan grilles and cab roofs, with a fair amount of the original roof colour still showing through albeit subjected to subtle tonal variation. If nothing else, this shows you how important a quality airbrush is, especially in 7mm scale.

11: Dry-brushing a small amount of Citadel 'Leadbelcher' on to the edges of the cab steps gives a convincing impression of wear where bare metal is exposed.

12: *The front end is the face of a diesel, and it's worth taking a bit of trouble to make it look its best. One of the falsehoods prevalent among modellers is that warning panels can and should be as heavily weathered as the rest of the loco. On the whole this isn't and never has been true – the panels are a safety feature and are regularly cleaned to ensure they remain visible to railwaymen on the track.*

13: *The first stage is to lightly airbrush the front end with 'Burned Black', concentrating on the buffer-beam area, which is always very grubby. Quite a bit of road dirt has accumulated on the cream band above it, but the discoloration on the yellow warning panel is minimal.*

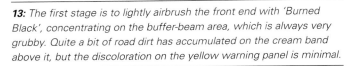

14: *One way of achieving these super-subtle effects is by removing the front section of the spray nozzle – technically called the crown cap – and spraying from close in with minimal air pressure. Be careful not to damage the exposed tip of the needle, though!*

15: *I've run some MIG 'Dark Wash' into the front-end details such as the footsteps and the marker-light housings. Dirt gets trapped in these areas and rapidly builds up, evading mechanical washing plants.*

16: *More than anything else it's the front end of a diesel or electric locomotive that draws the eye. A careful toning-down of the livery combines with dirt build-up in all the right places to create a convincing impression of a working locomotive.*

17: *Weathering this Brush Type 2 is all about the steady accumulation of detail, all of it derived from prototype photographs. You don't need to look at many images of these handsome engines in green livery before patterns begin to emerge.*

18: *Few locomotives epitomise their era so much as BR's transition-era diesels, even if many of them were dirty, unreliable and underpowered. The Brush Type 2s fared better and lasted longer than most, but they still couldn't pull the skin off a rice pudding.*

A 'J39' for Copenhagen Fields

Weathering techniques for 2mm locomotives present their own challenges. They are, like the models themselves, generally far less detailed than the standard that applies to the larger scales, but there is a great premium on restraint and finesse. I think it's about what you leave out so much as what you include. Anything clumsy really shouts out, especially in photographs – 2mm-scale models are generally shown at considerably larger than life size in books and magazines, whereas 7mm locos tend to be smaller – this fact helps considerably towards tightening the detail in O gauge, while it makes N gauge look coarser than it actually is.

In this section I'm going to take a Graham Farish LNER-liveried 'J39' and finish it as it would have looked a few months after delivery from Beyer Peacock in 1936. I needed to be specific here as – like the Gresley 'Pacific' *Papyrus* featured elsewhere in these pages – the engine was destined for the Model Railway Club's 2mm-scale layout 'Copenhagen Fields', which is set in the inter-war period. It would be seen alongside 'A4'-hauled streamliners such as the 'Silver Jubilee' – also launched in 1936 – which again creates a very specific timeframe.

Left: Although its tender-mounted drive system is a bit retro, there's nothing old-fashioned about the quality of finish on the Farish 'J39'. The complex lining-out is exquisitely rendered and is only a touch overscale in thickness and intensity. My challenge was to produce a workaday locomotive that was still relatively new.

1: I began by hand-brushing the tender with a thin mix of LifeColor 'Weathered Black' from the 'Rail Weathering' set. As soon as it was on, and before it had a chance to dry, I took it all off again using a flat brush dampened with acrylic thinners.

2: Acrylic paint dries so quickly that you only have a short time in which to work the paint. It is possible to slow down drying times using a retarder gel, but these additives can be expensive.

3: The same technique applied to the boiler – a thin paint mix on, and just as quickly taken off again to leave a fine residue collected in out-of-the-way places.

4: Working quickly soon begins to produce results. With its accumulation of finer streaks, the boiler is really starting to look the part – the running plate and boiler fittings will be treated separately.

5: The smokebox is one of the hottest parts of a steam locomotive, and even on an all-black engine it will usually be quite a different colour. LifeColor's 'Burned Black' (UA 736) has a warm tinge that is perfect in this application.

6: More 'Warm Black' on the cab roof, followed by a combination of 'Frame Dirt' (UA 719) and 'Weathered Black' on the locomotive and tender underframes.

7: The rear of the tender around the water filler is always a messy area, with water and coal dust combining in an acidic mix that encourages corrosion. Here I mixed the appropriate shade with paints from LifeColor's 'Rail Weathering' set – 'Sleeper Grime' (UA 721) and 'Brake Dust' (UA 724) – flooded on as a thickish wash. I used a similar mix on the tender front and toolboxes.

8: Footplates also become grubby very quickly. I like to scruff them up with MIG weathering powders, usually a combination of 'Industrial City Dirt' (P039) and 'Rubble Dust' (P234). Using tiny quantities, I stab them on with a stiff brush, then work away with the bristles to tone down the effect.

9: *I've added a touch of the same two weathering powders to the cab roof, followed by a dusting with 'Black Smoke'. If you use minimal quantities you can build up some incredibly subtle effects – as good as anything you can achieve with a quality airbrush.*

10: *MIG 'Dark Mud' powder (P033) works well with the LifeColor weathering shades I've used on the tender underframe, helping to suggest an accumulation of brake-block dust. I've used the same powder on the upper surfaces of the tender.*

11: *Through a combination of hand-brushed acrylic paint and weathering powders alone I feel I've achieved the look of a well-used but still cared-for locomotive. No 1856 would have been only a couple of years old at this period and will have been cleaned from time to time. There would have been little chance for corrosion to take a hold, or for any heavy build-up of oily dirt.*

12: *The final touches were to coal the tender with slack from the bottom of the scuttle and to paint the motionwork and tender axleboxes with AK-Interactive's 'Fuel Stains' to create that well-oiled look. Anything obviously overscale such as the handrails, stanchions and lubricator drive has been brush-painted with 'Burned Black' acrylic, which is a wonderful dark, neutral, slightly warm colour that somehow makes these things recede and even vanish. You might like to try this! It works!*

Southern electric units

I enjoy modelling the commonplace and humdrum, especially trains made up of endless numbers of MGR coal wagons, oil tanks, ballast hoppers and bogie bolsters. I like the repetition of everyday things but I also like to register small differences between notionally identical items of rolling stock. To the casual eye they all appear pretty much the same, but I like to see the tiny details that ensure many of them are, in fact, quite individual – variations in buffers and brake gear, axleboxes and pipework, livery and markings.

Weathering can also help build up these subtle variations. Adjacent vehicles will rarely be in exactly the same external condition but neither will they be radically different from one another. The same applies to locomotives, coaches and, to a lesser degree, multiple units. Here the diversity is less to do with individual vehicles in a set – which will tend for obvious reasons to be much of a muchness – than between the sets themselves. Stand on the end of any platform at any time in the last 60 years and you will see multiple units that, although externally identical and notionally painted in a common colour scheme, are subtly different from one another. Some will be acceptably clean, others decidedly grubby, the odd one immaculately ex-works.

Here I decided to ring the changes on a pair of Bachmann 2-EPB units to see how a few straightforward touches of weathering could make a subtle difference between sets that are otherwise identical. I haven't gone for anything too obvious and extreme, such as one unit ex-works and the other filthy, but concentrated instead on bringing out an everyday quality that was capable of subtle variations.

Right: Bachmann's 2-EPB is a brilliant model that captures the utilitarian quality of these units with considerable finesse. I've long had in mind a third-rail layout set in the 1950s/early '60s, so I wanted to show mine in the condition in which they'd have been around the time of the introduction of yellow warning panels.

1: Most of the weathering would be concentrated on the roofs and underframes, so it made sense to mask off the sides. I prefer a tape that doesn't have too aggressive a grip – the stronger ones can and do pull off transfers and even paintwork – but still has sufficient 'stick' to stop paint creeping under the edges. Kamoi is a good brand – it comes from Ripmax and is available in the better model shops – while Tamiya masking tape is easy to find and comes in a variety of thicknesses.

2: With the sides masked and checked for gaps, I began painting the roofs of the four cars. Doing them together makes sense, which is why they're lined up side by side on my painting turntable. The airbrush I'm using is an Iwata Revolution CR, which, with its 0.5mm head assembly, is capable of putting on a fair volume of paint in a short space of time.

3: Coach roofs are not one uniform colour but several, all closely linked and yet at the same time just about distinguishable. For the EPBs I used acrylic paints from LifeColor's 'Rail Weathering' set – 'Sleeper Grime' (UA 721), 'Roof Dirt' (UA 722) and 'Weathered Black' (UA 723). They are blended together with successive passes of the airbrush. For further subtlety I don't bother – at least in this instance – cleaning out the airbrush before recharging it with a fresh colour mix.

4: There is a similarly subtle gradation of colour on the ends, this time with the emphasis on 'Frame Dirt' (UA 719) from the same LifeColor set. All close-coupled stock has this blanket of road dirt over the ends, most of it thrown up by the wheels but with a darker tinge towards the roof.

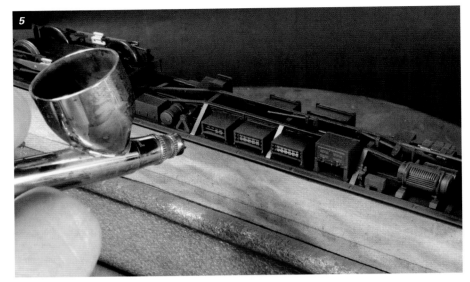

5: The detail on the underframe is exquisite, and careful weathering helps bring out its finer points. With 'Frame Dirt' still in the colour cup, I'm making a first pass over the resistances. Always allow some of the underlying colour to show through and don't be too concerned about a 100% uniform coverage – some patchiness is authentic.

6: Be careful to avoid the bald patches that invariably result from spraying from just one angle. If you spray in turn from above, below, left and right you'll get the paint where it wants to be. Use light coats and don't be too heavy on the trigger. Drifting on a second colour – 'Weathered Black' in this instance – adds visual interest and stops everything becoming too uniform.

7: Finally the masking tape can be peeled back to reveal the untouched coach sides. Subtle contrasts always work well in weathering and the one between the clean bodywork and grubby underframes and roofs is particularly effective – as well as being prototypical.

8: RTR coach bodies are often supplied in an odd-looking semi-matt finish that doesn't square with reality. Coach sides are always heavily varnished, so they look good fresh from the paint shop and for some months to come – while the Bachmann 2-EPB is shinier than most, it's still not enough to represent a recently ex-works vehicle. I masked off the roofs and underframes and sprayed Johnson's Klear floor polish over the bodysides to give a more prototypical 'freshly varnished' sheen to one of the sets. The windows aren't affected.

9: The other set retains its factory finish, suggesting that while it passes regularly through washing plants it's been a long time since it last saw the paint shop. With the cars lying on their sides, I ran a thin grey-brown enamel wash into the door panels and around details such as the hinges and bang plates. This serves to highlight relief detail through the creation of false shadows. The lower unit has yet to be treated, and the difference, although subtle, is marked.

10: Stepboards are made of wood, painted black, but they very quickly start to take on a much lighter hue. I represented this by brushing on small quantities of weathering powder, in this case MIG Productions' 'Rubble Dust' (P234), to give the right 'faded wood' effect. Work the powder well in, concentrating on the areas immediately below the doors. Don't get any on the bodywork or underframe.

11: *More detail weathering, this time around the axleboxes, which are usually caked with grease. Here I used LifeColor's 'Exhaust Oil Effect' (UA 261) dabbed on with a No 2 paintbrush. I did the buffer faces at the same time. A dark grey is much more effective than black.*

12: *There is not a great deal of difference between the condition in which these two units are presented, but it's there nevertheless – dirt build-up (or lack of it) on the front end, the degree of sheen on the bodywork, one with a yellow warning panel and the other without, one with horns, the other with a whistle.*

13: *It's small nit-picking differences like these that make modelling so interesting, even when the units are otherwise identical. One of the things that attracts me to modelling Southern Region EMUs is the bland uniformity and standardisation of much of what you see, making any small variation stand out.*

Kestrel: **filthy – and true to prototype**

Kestrel was the only one of the manufacturers' prototype diesel locomotives that I never saw. Its career on BR was brief and it operated in areas where – because steam had been eliminated from them – I felt no need to go. Being such a rare bird, *Kestrel* was infrequently photographed. Most of the published views were taken around the time of its introduction, and I was amazed some years back to find a photograph of it at Dairycoates shed in 1968 looking absolutely filthy. The cab fronts had been cleaned, together with the letters spelling out the name, but the rest of it was just covered in oil, road dirt and brake-block dust. This cried out to be modelled...

A trawl of the internet eventually unearthed two pictures of the other side of this magnificent machine, also at Dairycoates and taken at roughly the same time as the other one. At any remove, pictures showing both sides of a locomotive in the same timescale are not common – let alone when the subject is such a one-off. Although taken in very poor light, you could see that the cabs had been cleaned – but not quite so far back on one side – while the word 'Kestrel' was almost obliterated. This was all the stimulus I needed to make a start, a good 20 years after I'd decided a filthy *Kestrel* would be just the thing.

Using paints, powders and other materials to put across the essential qualities of a humdrum working locomotive primarily calls for observation. We need to think about what we want to convey, studying the prototype and trying to understand why things are the way they are. The weathering of *Kestrel* focuses on copying exactly what is seen in the prototype images. Total control of the airbrush is vital and for this project I used my Iwata HP-SB, which is capable of very fine, delicate work. The paint colours I used are very much a secondary consideration.

1: With its extraordinary colours and pristine grey roof, it's not easy to picture Heljan's 4mm scale model of Kestrel *as a working locomotive. The underframe is always the first area to pick up dirt, so I began the weathering process with a thin dusting of track colour – in this case a combination of Revell 'Matt Black' (No 8) and Humbrol 'Matt Leather' (No 62). Although the camera shows my airbrush spraying from quite an angle, you need to come in from all points of the compass (high, low, left, right) to be sure of getting a decent coverage.*

2: The airbrush is an Iwata HP-SP Plus, chosen because of its ability to put on fine wafts of paint and also because its offset colour cup gives me a great view of the work in progress. The drawgear and buffers can be treated in the same way as the bogies, working the airbrush from different angles to make sure everything is covered. Don't forget to add a big lump of compacted oil in the centres of the buffers.

3: The practice of cleaning diesel locomotives at both ends – but not in the middle – seems to have begun in the mid-1960s and continues to this day; I assume it relates to the need to make warning panels visible. To replicate this effect I started by masking off the left-hand end with a header card and spraying a thin, patchy coat of track dirt over the mid-section.

4: I did the same at the opposite end, again using the same two enamel colours but creating more of a brownish-grey mix. You don't want too definite an edge, so I feathered the paint off by airbrushing freehand, then built up the grime shades on the underframe and bodysides. I like to overlay a variety of paint mixes based on the same colours as before, but in varying proportions – some more black, some more brown – to emphasise the relief detail.

5: Note the gentle gradation of colour density in the weathering, again reflecting the patterns found on the prototype. This is where the fine control of the airbrush comes into its own – I don't think you could recreate this kind of effect by any other means, or with a budget airbrush. Now that I've created a definite edge I'm beginning to build up weathering on the lower bodysides.

6: *I've left the bodysides alone for now so I can start to fill in the roof. This is the same 'Matt Leather'/'Matt Black' mix as before, but with more of a preponderance of the latter. Again note the use of a header card to act as a spray mask. Once the basic colours have been blocked in we can start on the clever stuff, but for now I'm concentrating on achieving a good base coat as the basis for better things.*

7: *Here we're working along the roof, adding graduations of colour. I like to start with a mid-tone, then add a slightly darker colour and finally apply a lighter shade to emphasise form and create subtle highlights. Three modulations of the same basic colour would usually be enough to make a roof look subtly varied and hide the monochromatic livery colour.*

8: *Kestrel had large windows in the roof, which seem to have been kept fairly clean, as were the surrounding panels. While I was adding weathering to the mid-section of the roof I masked off this area, then later gave it a fine misting that toned down but didn't obscure the glass panels. You couldn't make up something like this in a month of Sundays, but this is exactly how Kestrel looks in the prototype reference photographs I was copying. Some feathering in and a fair bit of hand-finishing will make all the difference.*

9: *Now I've added a light coat of weathering with a spot more black in it, concentrating on the roof fans and the cab roof to emphasise form. Paradoxically the deeper recesses of the moulding still show up in unpainted grey, so these will need attention, as will the 'shadows' around the cab vents and other raised detail.*

10: *I've eliminated the glaring bald patches in the recessed detail by coming in close with my airbrush and filling in the gaps. This is one of several areas where a quality airbrush will score hands-down over a more basic model. You don't need saturation coverage, just sufficient paint to get down below the surface and into the little cavities such as around the roof horns.*

11: *These streaks running down the roof are sprayed by cutting a narrow slit in a business card, then spraying through it with the airbrush. If you hold the card tight up against the bodywork you get a sharply defined mark, but if you hold it further away the streak is more diffused. For best results you need a range of different effects.*

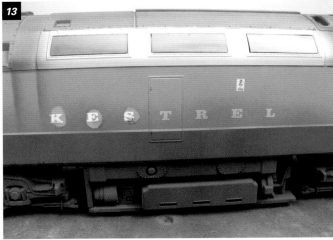

12: *The finish on this side of the locomotive was looking pretty good, but on the prototype the letters spelling out the name had at some point been cleaned. Recreating this effect was an essential part of the weathering project.*

13: *Using a small, stubby paintbrush well moistened with thinners, I began to dab the weathering paint off the individual letters. The part-cleaning of Kestrel hadn't been done very well, or even very consistently. I copied the individual shapes as best I could, using my brush to loosen the paint before dabbing up the residue with cotton buds and tissues.*

14: I gradually extended the areas that had been cleaned, exactly as per my reference photographs. Streaking and wipe marks were apparent and were duly replicated. Some of the patches were joined together. Finally, to tone down the exposed yellow paint and reduce the contrast, I added a light dusting of weathering over the top.

15: More attention with a damp brush breaks up the smooth airbrush finish. Oddly enough, I find upward movements work just as well as downwards, but until the paint has fully hardened – which takes several days – you need to be careful not to disturb areas you want to remain untouched, such as the underframe and the cantrail area.

16: The front end can also be improved by taking off some of the weathering, leaving grubby patches and streaking. With enamel paint you can continue to work on the finish for some considerable time after application – a good couple of hours and probably longer – but it's best to start roughing it up fairly soon after spraying.

17: With a few more dabs and wafts, we end up with this brute...

A Drewry shunter: mixed-media weathering in 7mm scale

As we saw with *Kestrel*, it's perfectly possible to weather a locomotive using enamel paint alone. It's also true to say that, right up to the time we produced my first Activity Media DVD, *Weathering Techniques*, I relied almost exclusively on enamels and a handful of weathering powders. That was about five years ago and it amazes me now to think how restricted my approach once was.

I think a lot of people are like that. Some ask me if I use enamels, or do I use acrylics, suggesting that to their way of thinking it's an either/or issue. The answer is, I use all sorts – whatever does the job best, whatever goes with what I already have, whatever happens to be to hand, whatever I've been given or recommended, whatever I feel like using. I'm not by nature a great experimenter, having the Taurean's faith in tried-and-tested methods, but I'm all for diversity in whatever form it comes – especially in a specialist field such as weathering.

My brief here was to repaint and weather a 7mm-scale Bachmann Brassworks Drewry shunter to represent a locomotive of the mid-1950s – a couple of years old, clean and yet grubby all at the same time, plenty of signs of use, oil everywhere. To achieve this effect I used quite a variety of materials. Some will be familiar to you, others quite new perhaps. What brings them together is their proven compatibility both in terms of material characteristics and colour coordination.

Above: The bland paintwork of the Brassworks locomotive disguises the underlying excellence of the product and the high level of detail. In this form it looks like a nice model, but no more than that. Out of the box, the amount of character on display is negligible.

1: A black loco was required – not least, because it would show up the dirt well – and I repainted the bodywork using an airbrushed coat of Humbrol No 85 'Satin Black' enamel. It's good practice to paint any inside corners first rather than try and fill them in later.

2: Once the paint in the corners was touch-dry I resprayed the rest of the bodywork, again using an Iwata Eclipse CS airbrush. With its 0.35mm nozzle, this is a great airbrush for fine detail work, but it still offers more than enough coverage to paint a 7mm loco in five or six passes.

3: I blackened the brightwork on the chassis using permanent markers. It's a lot quicker than gun blue and just as effective. I no longer use etching marker pens after I'd found they'd caused severe rusting on a set of Alan Gibson's steel-tyred driving wheels. I'd never had this problem before but I wasn't going to take the risk twice.

4: The cab interior has been repainted pale grey as per the prototype. I used BR 'Rail Grey' as I happened to be using some on another project at the time. I poked the airbrush through the unglazed windows and let rip – an awkward process. I'd almost finished the job when I discovered that the roof unscrews…

5: With the bodywork propped up on a foam cradle, I put a basic weathering mix on the area below the footplate. This part of a locomotive, coach or wagon tends to be pretty consistent in terms of overall colour and I can get much the same effect using either enamel or acrylic paint. If nothing else, this helps to ensure continuity with other models. When using acrylics I usually give a light coat of 'Frame Dirt' (UA 719) from LifeColor's 'Rail Weathering' followed by a mist of 'Burned Black' (UA 736) from the 'Black Rubber' set.

6: The same colours have been applied to the inner chassis. I use acrylics here to exploit their fast-drying properties, allowing me to start adding enamel washes and weathering powders within the hour. With enamel paints as the foundation, you'd have to wait until the next day at least. With the thin mists of paint that I've been using, by the way, there's absolutely no danger of gumming up the works or obscuring detail.

7: Graphics came from a Woodhead Transfers sheet dating back to the 1990s. I have a huge collection of transfers, many of them ancient, most of them dried-out, but all capable of being reactivated using Microsol or its less powerful stablemate, Microset. Cut out the image (Pressfix or Methfix, it doesn't matter), place it in position, press down gently, dampen with the setting solution, give a second application about a minute later, count to 20 and slide the backing paper away. Works every time. Check final position, then lightly dab down again.

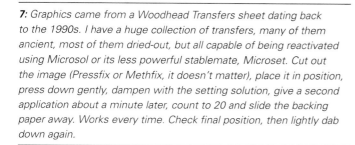

8: The core of the bodywork weathering focuses on creating an oily discoloration, which will initially be done using enamel washes. This will necessarily be very subtle. You can either prepare your own washes or use ready-mixed ones, such as these from the Adam Wilder range. I began by puddling on some 'Black Smoke Wash' (NL 01) using a wide, flat brush and allowing it to collect in corners. Avoid obvious brush marks but allow a measure of randomness to creep in.

9: While waiting for the first wash to dry I airbrushed the cab roof with LifeColor 'Burned Black' acrylic, then went over it again with a thin mist of 'Weathered Black' (UA 723) from the useful 'Rail Weathering' set. Cab roofs – on steam locomotives as well as diesels – are usually a pretty solid colour devoid of much by way of weathering patterns. I put more of the same on the bonnet top.

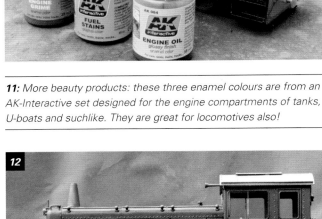

10: I added further washes from the selection I'd chosen, then left the paintwork to dry overnight. Inevitably there was some patchiness, so the following morning I lightly airbrushed some areas with a coat of 'Diesel Exhaust' (NL 31), which has the right smoky, sooty feel. Other areas were blended in with a touch of 'Burned Black' using an Iwata CM-C Plus airbrush, a wonderfully sophisticated tool that's ideal for this kind of fine detail work.

11: More beauty products: these three enamel colours are from an AK-Interactive set designed for the engine compartments of tanks, U-boats and suchlike. They are great for locomotives also!

12: You can see the result of playing around with those 'oily' colours below the footplate. Note the different finishes. The caked-on oil around the wheel centres is a particularly good weathering powder from the Adam Wilder range called 'Old Grease' (GP 11). Weathering at this level is about infinite nuances of shade and texture, each scarcely distinguishable from the last.

13: I used a more conventional technique to get the effect of ingrained dirt around the buffer-beam area – I made up a thickish wash of Revell 'Matt Black' enamel, applied with a clapped-out brush, then washed most of it off with white spirit to leave a stubborn residue in the nooks and crannies. Finally I blew some ComArt 'Burnt Sienna' over the lower part of the buffer-beam to represent road dirt.

14: The final stage of weathering is an endless round of touching up, correcting wonky numbers, spotting in paint chips and other minor adjustments. The key is knowing when to stop. Put the model down, go and do something else for a fortnight, then see what needs to be done. Just as when you're building a model, taking work-in-progress shots as you go along is a great way of picking up flaws that might otherwise have passed unnoticed.

15: Small, ugly engines always have terrific character, and the Drewry has it in spadefuls. The transformation from the blandness of the out-of-the-box model comes about purely through putting a dab or two of paint in the right places. Other than having had its cab windows glazed with two-thou Mylar, the actual model is exactly as it came out of the box.

A work-stained Beyer-Garratt

You'd need to be pushing 70 to have any memories of the LMS Garratts. I missed these huge, ungainly, instantly recognisable brutes by about a year – the last survivor featured in my *Observer's Book of Railway Locomotives* but not my first Ian Allan *Locoshed Book*. My disappointment was soon tempered by the discovery of bigger and better things such as 'Big Boys' and 'Challengers', but the Garratts had left an indelible mark.

Though I have the Kitmaster kit – still unmade – I've always yearned for something a bit more accurate. Over the decades I've been slowly building my way through the one-hit wonders of the locomotive world – from the 'Hush-Hush' and the Great Eastern 'Decapod' (both of which I never saw) right through to *Falcon*, *Lion* and *Duke of Gloucester* (all of which I did). I'm still hoping for Bulleid's 'Leader', but the arrival of the Heljan Garratt represented a further significant underlining in my 4mm scale fantasy spotting book.

Virtually all my weathering projects relate either to things I've seen or have good colour references for. Neither applies to the Garratt, so I had to rely on intuition, a couple of colour slides from the Colour Rail collection and the interpretation of black and white photographs. The outcome is a Garratt that looks like I imagine it should, had I become interested in railways a few months before I did.

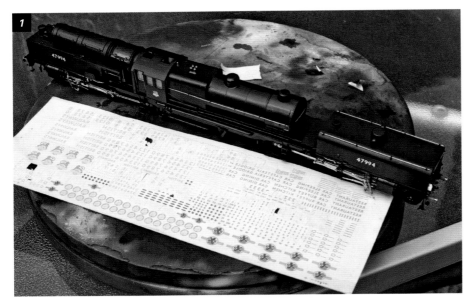

1: I added new insignia from an ancient sheet of PC Models BR steam-era lettering, still available via the HMRS. Long since dried out – I have no idea whether it's the Methfix or Pressfix type – it is easily reactivated by giving the letters a good soaking in Microsol once you've cut them out and moved them into position. You will need the 10-inch numbers and the smallest crest on the sheet. Both lions should face the chimney.

2: *Even in 4mm scale, an articulated locomotive 88 feet long is not the easiest thing to manoeuvre. To simplify working on the underframe, I inverted the model in a foam cradle, then gave the wheels and motion a light covering of LifeColor 'Frame Dirt' (UA 719), which is a good basis on which to build up subsequent effects. I used fast-drying acrylic paints throughout the initial stages.*

3: *To vary the tone I added a thin coat of LifeColor 'Burned Black' (UA 736) to selected areas. A warm, natural-looking colour, this harmonises well with 'Frame Dirt'. It's a great colour for making things vanish, such as overscale valve-gear components and clumsy handrails.*

4: *The next stage was to drift a thin mist of faded black over the upper works. To do this I used not one but four shades of black from LifeColor's 'Black Rubber' set, beginning with more 'Burned Black'.*

5: The upper parts of the locomotive were then painted with 'Dirty Black' (UA 731) and 'Worn Black' (UA 734), which are quite light in tone. I used 'Weathered Black' (UA 723) on the tank sides, followed by more 'Burned Black' on the smokebox. Where one shade ends and another begins is conjectural.

6: 'Burned Black' is a warm colour that suggests the heat of the smokebox quite well. To intensify the effect I overpainted it, when dry, with 'Dark Brown Filter' (NL 18), an enamel paint from the Adam Wilder range. Filters subtly change the character of the colours they're applied to, but are not really substantial enough to use as weathering paints in their own right. The airbrush is my Iwata Eclipse CS.

7: The best product I know for creating the effect of oily motionwork is 'Fuel Stains' (AK 025) from the AK-Interactive range. This is an enamel-based paint, applied with a No 3 brush. The acrylic paint beneath it won't lift because it's been given a good 24 hours to dry.

8: The exposed firebox areas of the Garratts were heavily burned – as they are on all steam locomotives. I used acrylic paints from LifeColor's 'Burned' set – all of them, in fact, as well as the indispensable 'Burned Black'. I like using this range of ready-mixed paints because the colours are very similar to those I mix myself!

9: To paint the firebox I used my Iwata Custom Micron CM-SB, which, with its 0.18mm-diameter nozzle, is the finest of all the airbrushes I own. It seems perfectly happy with neat LifeColor acrylics but it's not a tool I'd recommend to the beginner. With these very fine airbrushes – the HP-SB as well as the Custom Microns – paint preparation is all-important. The smallest lump can block that delicate plumbing.

10: After allowing several days' drying time, I started weathering the boiler and tank sides with enamel colour washes from the Adam Wilder range. I brushed them on by hand using a No 2 brush that was past its best, but still capable of coaxing the washes into subtle vertical streaks. Be careful to avoid any lines building up behind the handrails.

11: You can see how the effects are starting to develop. The colour variations are not great but they are there, as are hints of texture on the smokebox and around the coal doors on the bunkers. I did the whole loco with no more than a couple of brushloads of wash.

12: After the colour washes had dried I airbrush-blended certain areas to eliminate rough patches and give a layered effect. For this I went back to LifeColor's 'Burned Black' acrylic. The Iwata Custom Micron is a superb tool for this kind of touching-in work.

13: Final tints are added with weathering powders from several ranges. On the bodywork I used dabs of MIG's 'Black Smoke' (P023) and 'Dark Mud' (P033), together with Adam Wilder 'Old Grease' (GP 11), carefully smoothing and merging them during application. The distinctive orange discoloration on the cylinder covers is LifeColor's 'Yellow Tone' (PG 109).

14, 15, 16: *Fifty shades of grey: this extensive use of colour washes and weathering powders is a very American approach. I think I was subconsciously inspired by the some of the spectacular weathering I've seen on 'Big Boys', 'Alleghenies' and other articulated designs.*

Left: We start with two outwardly similar locomotives in the same livery. Freightliner's No 66612 Forth Raider is the original design, with three-part cab windows, long-range fuel tank, and yellow buffer-beams carried down to the air dam. No 66625 is the later low-emissions version with two-part cab windows, small fuel tank, extra bodyside door, larger grilles and other detail differences. It is one of only three low-emission 66/6s, and my model is based on a Bachmann 66/9. Both locomotives have been given additional detailing, and No 66612 has lost its Freightliner branding – since about 2004 the prototype has run in plain green.

Freightliner 66s: two of a kind?

A lot of modellers seem to give everything in their locomotive fleet the same weathering treatment, ignoring the fact that on real railways of any period or location the rolling stock will be in every kind of condition, from immaculate to utterly decrepit.

The need for variety is paramount. In this book, as in previous ones, I've intentionally shown locomotives in all kinds of external states – clean, grubby, bulled-up to the nines and absolutely filthy, with, I hope, all shades in between. This approach is even more desirable if you model the modern scene where the range of locomotive types and liveries is severely limited.

Whatever their interests, the chances are that most modellers will have more than one example of a particular class in their fleet. This applies whether your layout is populated by pannier tanks, 'Black Fives' or Bulleid 'Pacifics', and I think it works much better if you introduce a little diversity in terms of weathering treatment. Here we have a pair of Freightliner Class 66/6s that are differentiated not just by variation in their external condition but also by individual details related to the different batches they represent – one a low-emissions five-door model with the later pattern of cabside windows and light clusters, the other the earlier version.

1: I removed the Freightliner branding on No 66612 by gentle but sustained rubbing with a fibreglass brush. Having carefully cleaned off the resultant dust, I masked the two adjoining corrugated panels and resprayed them. Phoenix Precision's 'Freightliner Green' (P246) was far too dark, and the Railmatch version wasn't much better, so I had to mix it 60:40 with Revell 'Yellow Gloss' (310) to get a good match.

2: *With the loco inverted in a U-shaped length of foam, I brush-painted the wheels of both locos using LifeColor 'Frame Dirt' (UA 719). Use an old brush for this. After a while some brands of acrylic paint seem to start to clog and crystallise, making it difficult to spray them through an airbrush without blocking. When this happens, I relegate the paint to 'hand-brush only' status.*

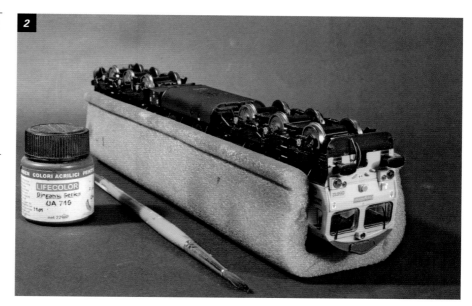

3: *Using a fresh jar of 'Frame Dirt', I've part-filled the colour cup of my Iwata TRN-1, and am adding a few drops of retarder, which will considerably slow down the drying time, making it possible to work the acrylic paint post-application, much as I do with slow-drying enamels. The exact proportion needed depends on the brand – I reckon on about 20-25% retarder.*

4: *The paint is now lightly sprayed over the bogies and frames, taking care to get good coverage among the many recesses and angles that characterise the running gear of a Class 66. To keep paint off the bodysides I used a simple card mask.*

5: *More 'Frame Dirt' is sprayed lightly on the obstacle deflector/snowplough. The cab ends of these locomotives are regularly washed, so there's no need to go to extremes and put grime all over the yellow paint.*

6: *With a No 3 candle-flame brush dipped in acrylic thinners, I'm now starting to brush off the still-wet underframe grime and work it into random streaks and smudges. Untouched airbrushing leaves everything looking far too neat and even.*

7: *The outcome: a patchy coverage of road dirt. The gradations are subtle and very far from dramatic, but they are plainly visible and accord exactly with prototype images. Real-life weathering rarely looks like airbrush weathering!*

8: I've now lightly misted over parts of the bogies with a 50:50 mix of 'Frame Dirt' and LifeColor 'Burned Black' (UA 736), which induces further tonal variety within a restricted palette.

9: Now for the silencer units, which, unlike the ones on these out-of-the-box Bachmann models, are neither silver nor red oxide. Like the wheelsets, they are rusty even when new and neither is ever painted. The first step is to mask off the surrounding area with tape.

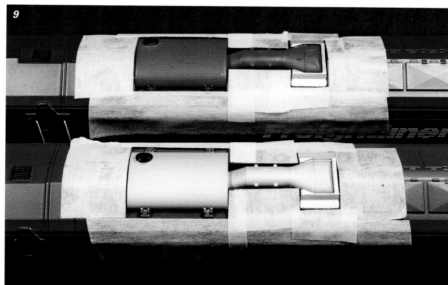

10: Once this is done, you can then spray the shadowy areas beneath and around the edges of the silencers with 'Burned Black'. Note how close in I'm working with my TRN-1 – a fine airbrush for delicate close-up work. Airbrush pressure is about 18psi.

11: Now I've started to fill in the main silencer/exhaust assembly with LifeColor 'Reddish Rust' (UA 908). This comes from the useful 'Rusty' combination set, which also includes complementary weathering powders.

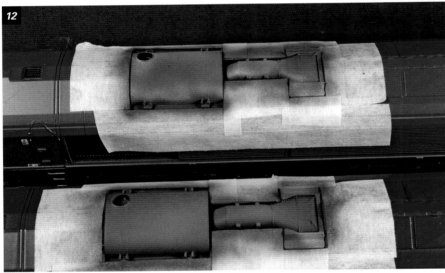

12: Corrosion is not one solid shade – certainly not on a Class 66 silencer. Here I've added delicate highlights using tiny quantities of 'Yellow Rust' (UA 909) from the 'Rusty' set.

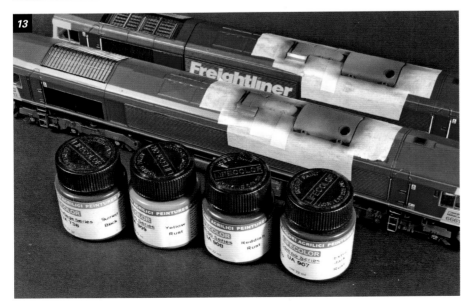

13: The final stage is to add some deeper tones using UA 907 'Extra Dark Rust'. A study of real Class 66s will reveal quite a variety of rust tones in this area – no two are quite alike. Any more than the four shades I've used here, however, will tend to overpower the result.

14: *There is always a lot of sooty build-up around the exhaust outlet on any main-line diesel, and the Class 66 takes this to extremes. Nothing beats an airbrush for this kind of effect and my medium here is plain Revell Matt Black (8) let down to spraying consistency but otherwise used straight out of the tin. Again, the 0.35mm head assembly on the trigger-action TRN-1 gives very precise control.*

15: *Now we can move on to pick out the roof detail and panel lines, suggesting both shadows and dirt build-up. For this I use not the black you might expect, but a thin, browny-grey wash – MIG 'Dark Wash' – which is an enamel-based paint thinned to exactly the right consistency for brushing on and brushing off again. You can, of course, always mix your own...*

16: *Because it's still wet in this view, the 'Dark Wash' is a bit more obvious than it will be when it's dried. I've put tiny quantities on a broad brush and worked this down the whole of the roof in vertical streaks.*

17: *The intention is to brush it all off, but of course you never will and the outcome is a delicate evocation of rain-washed paintwork – again, exactly what you see in photographs of real Freightliner '66s'. This kind of effect can only be recreated using hand-finishing techniques.*

18: *As with a passenger coach, the contrast between relatively clean bodywork and a heavily weathered underframe and roof really helps to bring a model to life. Far too many models have an all-over coat of weathering that rarely looks convincing – we can save that for railhead treatment trains.*

19: *I wanted No 66612* Forth Raider *to look altogether grubbier than No 66625, and I achieved this effect by putting on more weathering generally and in particular by airbrushing a quantity of 'Frame Dirt' over the bodysides to suggest the road dirt seen in photographs of Freightliner locomotives in a comparable condition. These marks of intensive usage offset the plainness of the debranded livery.*

20: MIG's 'Oil and Grease Stain Mixture' is a semi-gloss wash ideal for fuel tanks, bogies and steam locomotive underframes. It is brushed on in the quantity desired and left to dry. For definite and more pronounced streaks, use AK-Interactive's 'Oil Stains' and 'Fuel Stains'.

21: No 66625 is quite a clean locomotive, but the build-up of dirt on the underframe, fuel tanks and along panel lines helps to suggest that it works for a living. Note the oily areas around the fuel fillers and axleboxes, which further enhance this effect. I've eliminated the yellow axlebox covers – this is not a feature normally found on Class 66s unless they've been spruced up for a special occasion.

22: No 66612 Forth Raider reflects the condition of a locomotive that's been in intensive traffic use and hasn't been washed for some while. In winter these effects become even more marked and the green livery shows up the dirt to an impressive degree. The amount of weathering is quite heavy but nothing remotely like that on an RHTT locomotive.

Pushed to extremes

Even the very best finishers tend, in my experience, to stick with media they know will work for them. My preferred palette, as for many others, is a combination of Humbrol enamels and MIG powders, augmented by LifeColor acrylics. I have masses of other stuff that I've either been presented with or bought in the hope of salvation, but for the most part it sits in boxes, gently coagulating.

I've never been one to favour innovation for its own sake, but at the same time it pays to stay ahead of the game. My weathering inspiration always comes from the real thing; on the technical side, I pay more attention to what the armour and aviation guys are up to than to the timid, formulaic approach of most railway modellers. Instead of *RMWeb* or *MRJ*, it's *AFV Modeller* and *The Weathering Magazine* that float my boat.

It was here that I first saw the AK-Interactive range, and I thought it might be interesting to try out some of these specialised media alongside the everyday stuff I use, as well as taking an armour-modeller's approach to weathering a railway subject. AK-Interactive products are dearer and harder to find (you can buy online at www.ak-interactive.com, or click on the 'Dealers' link for a list of UK suppliers), but they are among the very best on the market and clearly do the job they're intended for. In the long run, though, no weathering product on earth can ever be a substitute for experience, manual skill and an educated eye.

Below: The AK-Interactive range is vast, encompassing both the conventional paints and powders shown here and a beguiling selection of specialised products for filtering, streaking and chipping the paint finish. These are what we'll be using in this article.

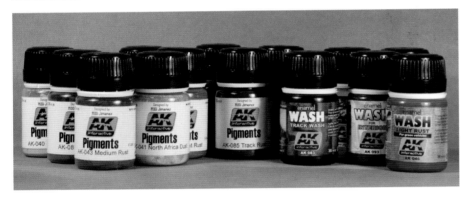

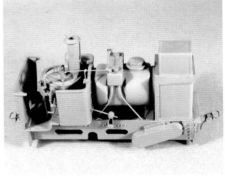

Above: Seen here in primer, this 7mm scale model of an 8-ton, 80hp Sentinel 'Industrial Locomotive' was built in New Zealand by Paul Berntsen. For those unfamiliar with these eclectic machines, there is a vertical boiler at one end, a set of pistons under a casing at the other, and a circular water tank in between.

1

1: I began by airbrushing the locomotive with a basic 'old rust' shade, for which Revell No 84 enamel always does very well. Described as 'Leather Brown' it has the necessary purple tinge.

2: To vary the tone in selected areas I added a second, more gingery coat, this time using 'Brown Streaking Grime' (AK 304) from AK-Interactive's Naval range of enamels.

3: Switching from my Iwata M1 single-action airbrush to a double-action CM-SB model, I turned to further, fresh-rust shades from LifeColor – UA 702 and 720 – modulated with 'Burned Black' (UA 734). I have no trouble applying acrylic paints over enamels and vice versa. Just allow adequate drying time – overnight if possible.

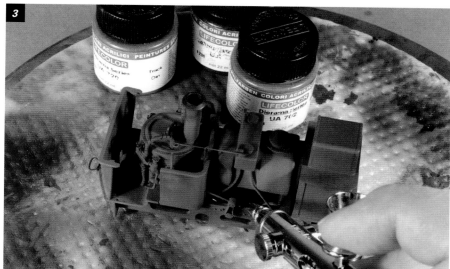

4: First thing next day I charged the M1 with AK's 'Heavy Chipping' solution and sprayed the cab and engine casing. This protects the rust shades beneath but allows me to chip away the top coat to suggest flaking paint. 'Worn Effects' has a similar function but the results are less extreme.

5: Immediately the 'Heavy Chipping' was dry I sprayed on two or three shades of faded black from LifeColor's 'Black Rubber' set. These give the bluish tinge that black acquires after prolonged exposure to the elements.

6: Using the ultra-fine CM-SB with its 0.18mm tip, the blue parts are oversprayed with one of AK's many streaking solutions – this is 'Rainmarks for NATO Tanks' (AK 074). It will further fade the body colour and create textures on the flat surfaces.

7: With a quarter-inch flat brush lightly dampened with white spirit, I'm diffusing the 'Rainwater' paint and coaxing it into subtle, barely discernible vertical streaks. This is far more effective than the heavy streaking many modellers employ because they think it looks like prototype weathering. It doesn't...

8: Having allowed a couple of hours' drying time, I'm prodding away at the faded blue-black top coat on the engine casing to reveal the rust beneath. Paint chips appear to happen almost at random but there is always a reason for it – corrosion is most marked adjacent to join lines, where water gets in.

9: For a more general flaking effect, splash the painted surface with water and stab gently at it with a stubby brush. The reaction with the chipping fluid will cause some of the topcoat to peel off in pleasingly random patterns. An undercoat of hairspray can produce similar results, but it's messy and unpredictable.

10: I painted the boiler unit separately. The pressure valves and other steam fittings are picked out in Humbrol Metal Cote 'Gunmetal' (27004) – not from a fresh can but using old, flat, dried-out paint dabbed on with a brush. This particular paint colour is now a lot more silvery than it used to be and for best results it needs to be let down 50:50 with Matt Black.

11: Old boilers are leaky, temperamental things that are prone to priming and other defects. I represented the characteristic seepage using 'Salt Streaks for Ships' (AK 306) applied with a No 2 brush. The off-white on the pipes represents asbestos lagging.

12: Handles and valves are usually brass, but on a locomotive in this condition they would be heavily tarnished. Revell RAF 'Dark Earth' (No 82) gives a far more realistic effect than metallic paint, and avoids that nasty 'fairground' look associated with the extremes of narrow-gauge modelling.

13: The wheels are the only part of the inner chassis that need weathering. LifeColor 'Frame Dirt' (UA 719) is my automatic choice for this, whether I'm weathering an elderly Sentinel or a brand-new Freightliner Class 66.

14: With the body removed from the chassis, I can take stock and decide what to do next. Although I work very quickly, these periods of contemplation and consideration are an important part of the weathering process.

15: The first thing is to enhance the rusting of certain areas using further washes and streaks from the AK-Interactive range. Load the brush well and flow the liquid on rather than painting with it. These paints are precisely the right consistency and you don't get tide marks or the unfortunate white bloom that comes from a liberal application of white spirit.

16: Detail weathering continues with irregular scrapes along the edges. I'm using a small pad of Scotch-Brite abrasive dipped in acrylic paint and wiped almost dry before applying.

17: Behind the oval casings are chains carrying the drive to the wheels. You can represent the inevitable oil leaks with AK's 'Engine Oil' (AK 084) and a couple of streaks of Humbrol Metal Cote 'Gunmetal' let down with Matt Black.

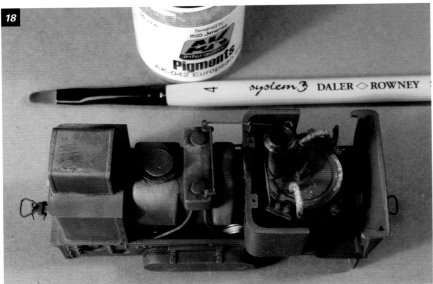

18: A dab or two of AK 042 'European Earth' pigment represents spillage from the sandbox located on top of the water tank.

19: I've stroked the drum-like water tank with AK's 'Salt Streaks', painted the top of the chimney matt black with dried-out Metal Cote 'Gunmetal', and airbrushed a fine spatter of mud (Humbrol 110 'Natural Wood') along the lower chassis using the lowest air pressure I could set – about 8psi.

20: *Once work on the boiler and cab was finished I could fit the roof, turning the diminutive narrow-gauge Sentinel from a convertible to a coupé model. The roof was given the same rusting/chipping treatment as the rest of the locomotive. Note the steam whistle.*

21: *I distressed and pitted the roof as before, this time using the gentler 'Worn Effects' and a sootier shade of black, LifeColor's 'Burned Black' (UA 734). In 7mm scale, textures are very visible; in the smaller scales, it's easy to exaggerate them, so I don't normally bother.*

22: *A touch of Metal Cote 'Gunmetal' on the badly corroded handrails/roof supports completes the job. If you lightly polish the pigment with your fingers or a cotton bud it gives a patina of well-rubbed metal with a subtle hint of greasiness – exactly what you'd find on a locomotive.*

It's worth looking at this locomotive from a variety of angles to study the range of effects that have been built up. Weathering the way the armour and aviation modellers do it is about the slow, patient accumulation of detail, layer upon layer, and in 7mm scale the flayed, rusting paintwork of this elderly narrow-gauge locomotive offers the perfect opportunity to try out techniques not normally seen on British locomotive models.

'T9' and 'Bulldog': all bulled up and ready to go...

Railways constantly present surprises, and one of the most unlikely motive power combinations I've encountered was the use of a Southern 'T9' and a GWR 'Dukedog' on the Shrewsbury to Towyn leg of a Talyllyn Railway special from Paddington in 1956. Though I've only seen photographs, the contrast between the sleekly curvaceous 'Greyhound' and the lumbering outside-framed 'Dukedog' was irresistible. Many years later the availability of high-quality RTR models enabled me to recreate such a pairing in 4mm scale.

Towards the end of their lives, elderly locomotives were often cleaned up for special workings, or simply because they were a local pet. There was no hiding the bumps, scrapes and patches that result from a long working life, but the sheds did their best – often with engines that hadn't seen a paint shop in years – to make them presentable.

I found inspiration in old *Railway Roundabout* footage of locomotive classes –including both of these – that had plainly been cleaned up for the camera. In this case the 'T9' is in better overall condition, with polished brightwork and the then new BR crest, whereas the 'Dukedog' shows evidence of a hard life amid the Cambrian mountains, one that oily rags and paraffin can never quite eradicate. Both, nevertheless, are far cleaner than the average British Railways locomotive of the mid-to-late 1950s and are a credit to the depot staff who prepared them for their day of glory.

Above: The two locomotives side-by-side in out-of-the-box condition. Though it doesn't take much to turn them into bulled-up, enthusiasts' special condition, the key factor is restraint. It's very easy to go over the top when making an engine dirty, but presenting them in clean condition takes a lot of care.

1: Although this 'T9' is going to be a very clean locomotive, initially I'm going to tone down some of the traditionally grubby areas around the wheels and underpinnings with LifeColor 'Burned Black' acrylic (UA 738). I'm using my Iwata Custom Micron SB for this because of the phenomenal delicacy of which this airbrush is capable.

2: More 'Burned Black' goes on the smokebox. This is always a different colour of black from the rest of the boiler and, since the latter is going to be pretty clean, I need to emphasise the point. Once again, the CM-SB does the honours.

3: I've put some 'Burned Black' on the top of the tender and now I'm adding tints of 'Extra Dark Rust' (UA 907) around the coal rails and other areas where corrosion would begin to take a hold. The colours need to be subtle here, and the blending discreet. If you haven't got a high-end airbrush, weathering powders work pretty well, but you have to be careful not to overdo it.

4: Highlights have been added using 'Yellow Rust' (UA 909). See how different the colours look on the white spray mask – a business card – on the left. I will add further rust variations in due course using weathering powders, which harmonise well with the LifeColor acrylics.

5: Even an airbrush as good as the Custom Micron can't compete with the subtlety of weathering powders lightly brushed on. Here I used just two colours, both from the AK-Interactive range. The combination of different weathering techniques is the way to achieve success and believability.

6: Prior to coaling the tender I added water spillage around the tank filler. There are many ways to do this – gloss varnish is probably the simplest – but one of the most convincing is 'Murky Waters' from the Adam Wilder range (NL 34).

7: I wanted the tender, cabsides and splashers to have a highly polished look, which I achieved by brushing on Johnson's Klear floor polish. Rather than spraying it on I use an old a half-inch flat paintbrush because the surface, when dry, will not be totally smooth – this helps create a desirable 'sheet metal' look. Two coats of Klear are normally sufficient.

8: I've brushed the boiler and firebox with a dark enamel wash – 'Black Smoke Wash' (NL 01) from the Wilder Nitroline range. This tones down the paintwork to give a further selective rendition of black. Already the locomotive is looking very different from the out-of-the-box RTR model with its uniform semi-matt finish and bright lining.

9: Final detail weathering follows familiar patterns. The brightwork has been toned down with black weathering powder, which I've also used sparingly on the cab roof, running plate, footsteps and smokebox. The 1956 BR crest (PC Models transfer) is the early, heraldically incorrect version with both lions facing forward.

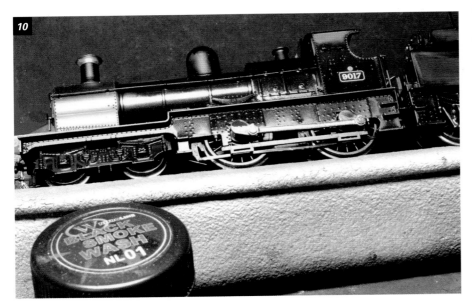

10: *I weathered the 'Dukedog' in quite a different way. To contrast with the smooth finish of the 'T9' I wanted to create the effect of old, pitted paintwork that has been cleaned with rags and paraffin. The first step is to brush a dark grey wash – 'Black Smoke Wash' once more – over much of the locomotive, and allow it to find its own way into corners and around detail.*

11: *Then, after allowing the paint to harden for half an hour, I took much of it off again with an assortment of flat brushes, lightly moistened with white spirit. I wanted a purposeful randomness, aping the routine discolorations and streaks that you'd find on a real locomotive.*

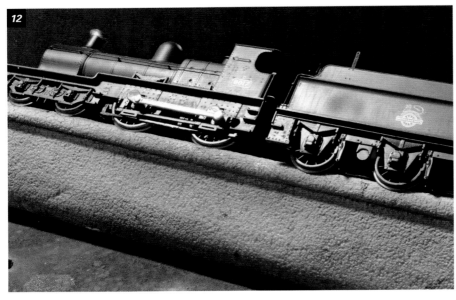

12: *This is how the wash looks the following morning, once the paint has been left overnight to harden off. It will form an undercoat for the 'cleaning' that I want to give this loco. I'm pleased with the arbitrary patterns that have formed – which in fact are anything but – and the overall matt finish was something I'd anticipated.*